DATE DUE			

Map from Goode's World Atlas
© 1993 by Rand McNally, R.L. 93-S-40

GOSLAVIA
Gusinje
Shkodr
Lezha
Debar
Skopje
Ohrid
Prilep
Bitola
Korça
Ædhessa
Katerini
Véroia
Konispol
Ioánnina
Párga
Árta
GREECE
Agrínion
Mesolóngion
Pátrai (Patras)
Amaliás
Píriros
Kalamái
Sparti (Sparta)

NOS EMINE

BULGARIA

Sofia
Plovdiv
Haskovo
Svilengrad

Edirne

Kavarna
Balčik
Varna
Burgas
Ahtopol

Black Sea

Map from Comprehensive World Atlas
© 1993 by Rand McNally, R.L. 93-S-40

KEREMPE BURNU İNCE BURUN
İnebolu Sinop
BAFRA BURNU

Istanbul
(Constantinople)

Ankara

TURKEY

İzmir
(Smyrna)

CYPRUS
Nicosia (Levkosía)

CRETE
(GREECE)

M e d i t e r r a n e a n   S e a

LEBANON
Beirut
(Bayrūt)
Damas

ISRAEL
Tel Aviv-Yafo
Jerusalem

(A) Golan Heights area. Occupied by Israel since
    1967. Unilaterally annexed by Israel, 1981.
(B) West Bank area. Unilaterally annexed by Jordan, 1950.
    Occupied by Israel since 1967. Status to be determined.
(C) Gaza Strip. Occupied by Israel since 1967.
    Status to be determined.

Alexandria
(Al Iskandarīyah)

Port
Said
(Būr Sa'īd)

Cairo
(Al Qāhirah)

EGYPT

LIBYAN PLATEAU

QATTARA
DEPRESSION
-436

Siwah
(Siwa)
(Oasis)

SARIR
CALANSCIO

WESTERN DESERT

SINAI
PENINSULA

Suez

Red Sea

Longitude East of Greenwich

Enchantment of the World

CYPRUS

By Mary Virginia Fox

Consultant for Cyprus: Alex G. Papadopoulos, Ph.D., Geography Department, DePaul University, Chicago, Illinois

Consultant for Reading: Robert L. Hillerich, Ph.D., Professor Emeritus, Bowling Green State University; Consultant, Pinellas County Schools, Florida

CHILDRENS PRESS®
CHICAGO

A young man with an elaborate shoe-shine stand waits for customers.

Project Editor: Mary Reidy
Design: Margrit Fiddle

Picture Acknowledgments
AP/Wide World Photos: 34, 36, 41 (2 photos), 43, 45 (2 photos), 46, 55, 56 (2 photos), 57, 58, 60
Lee Boltin: 4, 9, 11, 12, 14 (2 photos), 15 (2 photos), 16, 68 (2 photos), 69, 71, 72 (left), 74, 75, 78, 79, 81, 83 (bottom), 84 (right), 85 (2 photos), 86 (bottom), 87, 88 (2 photos), 89 (left and bottom right), 90, 91 (2 photos), 94, 96 (top and bottom right), 98 (top and bottom right), 103, 104 (2 photos), 105, 107, 110, 111 (2 photos), 112
Historical Pictures Service: 19 (2 photos), 20, 21 (right), 23, 28 (left), 33
North Wind Picture Archives: 21 (left), 24 (left)
Photri: 5, 8, 10, 18, 22 (left), 24 (right), 28 (right), 30, 39, 62, 65 (left), 66 (2 photos), 73, 76, 80, 82, 83 (top), 84 (left), 89 (top right), 93, 95 (2 photos), 97, 98 (bottom left), 102, 108 (2 photos); © **Jacqui and Peter Sanger,** 6
Tony Stone Worldwide/Chicago: © **Brian Seed,** Cover, 22 (right), 63, 64, 65 (right), 96 (left), 100 (2 photos); **George Chan,** 72 (right), 86 (top)
SuperStock International, Inc.: © **Rodney Bond,** 101
UPI/Bettmann Newsphotos: 49 (2 photos), 51
Len W. Meents: Maps on 58, 86, 95
Courtesy Flag Research Center, Winchester, Massachusetts 01890: Flag on back cover
Cover: Omodhes farmer with grapes in basket

Library of Congress Cataloging-in-Publication Data

Fox, Mary Virginia.
  Cyprus / by Mary Virginia Fox.
    p.   cm. — (Enchantment of the world)
  Includes index.
  Summary: Presents the geography, history, and customs of the divided Mediterranean island of Cyprus.
  ISBN 0-516-02617-8
  1. Cyprus—Juvenile literature. [1. Cyprus.]
I. Title. II. Series.
DS54.A3F68   1993   93-755
956.93—dc20   CIP
                                                     AC

The city of Lefkara

TABLE OF CONTENTS

Khrysokhou Bay in northeast Cyprus

Chapter 1

THE LAY OF THE LAND

Cyprus has a place in world history out of all proportion to its size. Although the third-largest island in the Mediterranean, behind Sicily and Sardinia, its land area is less than 3,572 square miles (9,251 square kilometers). At its greatest length the island stretches 128 miles (206 kilometers), and its maximum width is 75 miles (121 kilometers). It is roughly about the size of the Caribbean island of Puerto Rico, but Puerto Rico has more than five times as many people.

Cyprus is situated in the eastern corner of the Mediterranean Sea, easily accessible from Europe, Asia Minor, and the Middle East. In ancient times its neighbors—Greece, Turkey, and Egypt—developed some of the grandest civilizations that the world was ever to know. Much of Cyprus's heritage comes from this grandeur.

Human settlements existed on Cyprus as early as 5800 B.C. Its timber and mineral resources were a source of wealth to early traders, but wealth was bound to attract enemies as well as peaceful settlers. Cyprus has long been regarded as a possession of value, and conquerors often have come to collect the prize.

During most of its recorded history, the island has not been ruled by its native inhabitants. Since the fourteenth century B.C. it has been colonized successively by Mycenaeans, Ionians,

Roman ruins at Salamis

Phoenicians, and Persians. It was captured by the Egyptian Ptolemies, later annexed by Rome, and attacked by the Saracens. Between A.D. 1192 and A.D. 1489 Cyprus was ruled by a dynasty loyal to the pope in Rome, after which it was captured by the Republic of Venice. The island was incorporated into the Ottoman (Turkish) Empire in 1572. In its final phase of colonial history, Cyprus became part of the British Empire. British rule lasted from 1878 until independence in 1960.

Each of these civilizations left on the land some physical reminders of its influence. But in spite of the succession of foreign rulers, Cyprus retained its identity. In the year 1960 official independence was finally granted, when the island became known as the Republic of Cyprus. Even then not all Cypriots asked for their freedom. Many wished to keep their ties to Greece or to Turkey. Today Cyprus is divided between two cultures, Greek and Turkish, and two religions, Christian and Muslim.

The Troodos Massif is the larger mountain range in Cyprus.

CLIMATE

The warm Mediterranean climate, which is rather dry but with winter rainfall, is good for agriculture. Altitude and, to a lesser extent, distance from the coast govern the extremes of weather. Summer temperatures in the lowlands can be uncomfortably hot. For those who can afford a relief, some of the villages in the Troodos mountains have been developed as resort areas. Cyprus has long been known to tourists as the land of sunshine. During the six summer months, there is an average of eleven and one-half hours each day of cloudless weather.

THE LAND

The island is dominated by two mountain ranges. The larger and more extensive of the two is the Troodos Massif (mountain

A meteorological station at the top of Mount Olympus

range), which lies in the southwestern half of the island and rises to a maximum height of 6,403 feet (1,952 meters) on Mount Olympus. The Kyrenia range to the north and east is much lower, rising to only 3,360 feet (1,024 meters), but its jagged cliffs form a needle-sharp ridge that is considerably more spectacular. Its lofty crags are separated from the sea by a narrow belt of fertile land. Between the mountain ranges lies the plain of Mesaoria, meaning literally "between the mountains." This is the agricultural heart of Cyprus.

The Troodos Massif occupies around one-third of the island's surface—approximately 1,190 square miles (3,082 square kilometers). The area is sparsely inhabited along its upper slopes because of the rocky terrain. However, on the lower hills there are orchards of peach, plum, apricot, and almond trees.

The two ranges had a markedly different geological beginning.

An eroded area in the Kyrenia range

Whereas the Troodos Mountains were formed by molten igneous rock from early volcanic activity, the Kyrenia range is a narrow limestone ridge lifted out of an ancient sea.

Over many centuries the forests that once covered the area have been cut, allowing rain to wash away the topsoil. This has had a devastating effect on the island's drainage system. The water cannot soak into the compacted and eroded surface, so there is no moisture during the dry season.

Even the rivers that rise in the Troodos Massif and spread in all directions have a limited effect on the water table. Only during the rainy season do they fill with water. The Yialias and the Pedhieos, two rivers that drain eastward across the Mesaoria plain, become dry, cracked channels in summer. Wells are not able to reach a water source unless they are drilled to great depths.

The Mesaoria is the agricultural heartland of the country.

Many crops are irrigated.

Wheat and barley crops depend on rainfall. Other crops are grown with irrigation. This broad central plain was once covered with heavy forest. Timber was a valuable resource in ancient times, as shipbuilders prized the tall trees that were used to make the ships that sailed from one end of the known sea to the other.

Nicosia, the capital, is not built on the coast. Aside from a few seaport towns, the coastline of Cyprus is empty of people. The fresh drinking water in the mountains brought settlers inland from the coastal ports.

In the past Cyprus was not a maritime nation, as one would expect from its position on the map. The island simply served as a port for other nations. Today, through favorable government taxation incentives, shipping has become an important part of the economy. Cyprus now has the world's seventh-largest maritime fleet with two thousand ships sailing under its flag.

Chapter 2
THE WEALTH OF COPPER AND BRONZE

ANCIENT HISTORY

Archaeologists have found traces of humans living on the island as early as the Neolithic Era (New Stone Age), around 5800 B.C. It is not hard to draw an accurate picture of what life was like in those days. The study of tools and skeletons suggests that people had learned to till the land and raise animals for food. Small figurines of fertility goddesses show that the people had some kind of religious beliefs.

Tools made of obsidian, a glossy black stone not native to the island, prove that even these earliest people had some contact with the outside world. (The nearest sources of obsidian are in present-day Turkey and the island of Mylos in the Aegean Sea.) The northern coast of Cyprus is just forty miles (sixty-four kilometers) from what now is Turkey. The design of their houses was similar to those built on the mainland not so far away. Pottery was as yet unknown, but skillfully sculpted stone vessels were part of household remains.

In the earliest days, settlements were found only along the coastline. The island's central plain was probably too thickly

Excavations at Khirokitia have unearthed a Neolithic settlement (above) from about 6800 B.C. An idol (right) found at Khirokitia is in the Cyprus Museum in Nicosia.

wooded to make clearing of the land practical. The oldest site that has been excavated is at Khirokitia, some twenty miles (thirty-two kilometers) east of present-day Limassol. Here, archaeologists have found several layers of settlements that were built on the same site, one on top of another, over many years. Today one looks out over green fields dotted with olive trees, while shepherds tend their flocks of orange-brown goats, perhaps not so different a sight from that enjoyed by the first settlers.

The homes these early people built were round, beehive-shaped, and made of rubble, baked mud-brick, and wood on a stone foundation. The houses were built close together and fronted on a raised main street that ran straight up the hillside. Under the homes' stone foundations the villagers' burial places have been found. Skeletons were laid out side by side, knees bent, arms folded.

Tools (left) and a pitcher (right) from the Bronze Age

Today many of the stone axes, vessels, and idols found at the site have been transferred to the Cyprus Museum in Nicosia.

THE AGE OF COPPER AND BRONZE

The Chalcolithic period followed the Neolithic and lasted from about 3000 B.C. until 2300 B.C. This age was characterized by the discovery of copper, the island's chief mineral resource. This brought about a great surge in trade with Anatolia (now Turkey) and Egypt, and later with other Mediterranean communities. The island grew in prosperity as a result. New towns were founded, among them Erimi, Lapithos, and Kythrea. Little remains of these once-bustling communities today.

Working with copper, the early artisans found they could strengthen their product by adding other substances, particularly tin. The result was an even more durable product, bronze. The Bronze Age, from about 2300 B.C. to 1050 B.C., brought continued prosperity to the island.

15

Remains of the settlement known as Engomi/Alasia

DEFENDING THEIR PROSPERITY

By 1500 B.C. Cyprus was entangled in wars of international conquest between Egypt and the rebellious states of Syria, Mesopotamia, and Phoenicia which had once been conquered by Egyptian pharaohs. For its own safety, Cyprus sought the protection of Tethmesis III, one of Egypt's greatest rulers. The Egyptians promised they would come to the aid of the island if it were attacked by other neighbors. In return Cyprus agreed to sell its copper and other goods only to Egypt.

For the next hundred years Cyprus was under the rule of Egypt. There were few complaints and many cultural benefits. The protective agreement brought wealth to the island, as evidenced by the appearance of Egyptian scarabs and other jewelry found in Cypriot tombs of the day.

At this time the principal port for commerce was known as Engomi/Alasia. It was about five miles (eight kilometers) north of present-day Famagusta. Scholars estimate that between ten thousand and fifteen thousand people lived there, a large city for this age of rural culture. Engomi/Alasia later suffered from floods, fires, and earthquakes, and was abandoned in the eleventh century B.C. There are still signs of the massive walls of the city, with some stone blocks weighing as much as sixty tons (almost fifty-five thousand kilograms).

GREEK HERITAGE

With the rise of the Mycenaean and Minoan civilizations, the commercial supremacy of Egypt was challenged. Trade with the European and Asiatic mainlands increased. Egypt's monopoly of trade with Cyprus was no longer enforced. It was during the peaceful time of greatest prosperity, from about 1400 B.C. to 1250 B.C., that Greek merchants from the west first became frequent visitors in search of copper. Traders from the northeastern section of Greece began to settle in large numbers. By the end of the Trojan Wars, traditionally dated about 1184 B.C., more Greeks were searching for a peaceful place to settle.

These early immigrants brought their Greek language with them and introduced a system of money exchange with individualized scrip that greatly simplified trade. Each merchant established his own mark, which was pressed into clay tablets to identify the goods belonging to him, even when included in a large shipment of goods belonging to many traders.

Alashiya was an early name for all of Cyprus. Enkomi, built at the mouth of the Pedhieos and Yialias rivers, was the principal Cypriot city during the third period of the Bronze Age. Salamis was built near the site of Enkomi in the fifth century B.C. Before

The legendary birthplace of Aphrodite, the Greek goddess of love and beauty

long the colonists spread to other parts of Cyprus. These people were the early ancestors of the Greek Cypriots who inhabit the island today.

Imports had an effect on almost every form of Cypriot art. The potter's wheel was introduced. Seal engraving, gold jewelry, work in ivory, and faience (glazed earthenware) have been found in many of the archaeological sites of Cyprus's port cities.

Greek poets and playwrights in later ages frequently mentioned Cyprus. Aphrodite, the Greek goddess of love and beauty, was said to have been born from the sea foam on the island's west coast. One of the most important temples to honor the goddess of love was built at Paphos. Aphrodite is mentioned by the Greek poet Homer in both the *Iliad* and the *Odyssey*. The Cypriot king, Kinyras of Paphos, is also part of the story.

Over the years there was bound to be fluctuation in the course of progress. Some trade was lost with the introduction of iron tools and weapons, which replaced the bronze and copper that

*Sargon II (left) and a Phoenician fleet
on a voyage of discovery (above)*

Cyprus had provided. But by this time Greek culture had long been established on the island, and there was no chance that Cyprus would be abandoned.

An important influence from the east came about 800 B.C. with a settlement of Phoenicians. Although concentrated at Kition (the modern city of Larnaca) on the southeast coast, the Phoenicians spread out over other areas as well. They were the great shipbuilders and mariners of the day. Until the later arrival of the Assyrians, they shared political control of the islands with the Greeks.

EARLY GOVERNMENT

Cyprus was composed of at least seven independent kingdoms, called city-states, until they were conquered by the Assyrian king, Sargon II. For one hundred years Cyprus was officially under the command of Sargon II and his successors, although a great deal of power in domestic affairs was given to the Cypriot rulers of the former city-states. The Cypriot kings were religious as well as secular leaders.

Alexander the Great in the Battle of Issus

Assyrian power and influence began to decline near the end of the seventh century B.C., because of the tremendous fleet of warships commanded by the Egyptian pharaohs. The combined fleets of Phoenicia and Cyprus were defeated by the Egyptians, yet an even greater power was soon to take over.

Trade in the area came to an abrupt halt in the fourth century B.C. when Egypt was conquered by a powerful army of Persians (present-day Iranians), whose homeland was much farther to the east past the forbidding Arabian Desert. Cypriot military forces were forced to pay allegiance to Persia. Cyprus was made part of the fifth *satrapy*, or "province," of King Darius. At this time the city-kingdom of Salamis outshone the others in wealth and splendor. It was under the leadership of Onelsilos of Salamis that an unsuccessful revolt was mounted against the Persians in 498 B.C.

Cyprus was caught in the middle. The island tried to gain its independence by signing treaties with the more important powers of the day, but it never was entirely free. Persian power came to an end only after Alexander the Great decisively defeated the Persian army at the Battle of Issus in 333 B.C.

Alexander the Great at the seige of Tyre (left) and Cicero, the Roman orator (above)

Cyprus was granted self-government in return for helping Alexander at the siege of Tyre (Sur in present-day Lebanon). But after only ten years, at the death of Alexander in 323 B.C., the agreement was ended. Alexander's heirs fought over Cyprus for several years until in 294 B.C. it was taken by Ptolemy, one of Alexander's generals, who had established himself as king of Egypt.

Under the rule of the Ptolemies, which lasted for about two and a half centuries, the city-kingdoms of Cyprus were abolished and a *Hellenistic kingship*, an ancient Greek form of government, was established. It was a period of civil war, which ended only after Cyprus was taken over by the Romans.

ROMAN INFLUENCE

At first Rome governed the island as part of the province of Cilicia (a section of present-day Turkey). For a time Cyprus had the distinction of being ruled by the famous Roman orator, Cicero.

Roman ruins at Paphos (left) and Salamis (right)

With peace finally restored, prosperity returned. Mines were reopened and roads, harbors, and public buildings were built by the Romans.

The island was divided into four districts: Amathus, Lapithos, Paphos, and Salamis. Although Paphos was made the capital, Salamis remained the center of culture and education. An earthquake destroyed much of the city in 15 B.C., but Emperor Augustus had it rebuilt in grand Roman style. However, four hundred years later an earthquake once again demolished past glories, and this time Salamis was abandoned to the drifting coastal sand that eventually covered it until twentieth-century archaeologists dug deep into the ruins.

Chapter 3

CHRISTIANITY COMES TO CYPRUS

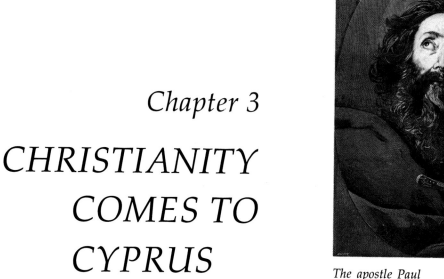

The apostle Paul

CHRISTIANITY

The introduction of Christianity to Cyprus came about during the rule of the Roman Emperor Claudius. It is said that the apostle Paul landed at Salamis in A.D. 45 accompanied by Barnabas, a convert to Christianity and an apostle. Barnabas was a native of Salamis, of Greek Jewish parentage. Paul and Barnabas converted the Roman proconsul who was in residence at Paphos. Thus Cyprus became the first area of the Roman Empire to be ruled by a Christian.

It was harder to change the customs of the people at large. Pagan beliefs persisted. Aphrodite was worshiped by many. According to legend, Barnabas was offended by the nakedness of young men and women athletes whom he saw competing during a pagan festival. As punishment he called down a thunderbolt that buried many of the participants in a landslide.

Constantine the Great (left) and the tomb of St. Barnabas (right)

It was at this time that large numbers of Jews from Palestine began to swell the already considerable Jewish population along the eastern coast. In the year A.D. 115 a Jewish revolt spread to Egypt and Cyprus. The destruction in Cyprus was worse than anywhere else. Led by Artemion, the entire gentile population of Salamis was massacred. By the time the future Roman Emperor Hadrian stopped the revolt, the Libyan consul, cavalry leader Lucius Quinctus, and some 240,000 other people had been killed. A decree was passed forbidding any Jew, on pain of death, to set foot in Cyprus. It was many years before any Jewish communities were reestablished.

Meanwhile the Christian religion was slowly gaining ground. The poor of the cities took hope in the humanitarian practices of a religion that gave hope to the poor. The pagan gods and goddesses of the past were linked, in thought at least, with the wealthy who lived in luxurious villas. Another strong influence came from a large number of Christians who were transferred to the island from the mines in Palestine. They came to find freedom and with freedom they exhibited an ardent desire to convert others. In A.D. 313 the Edict of Milan proclaimed equal rights for all religions. The Roman emperor at the time, Constantine the Great, declared Christianity to be the official religion of the Roman Empire in 333.

Soon the power of bishops was consolidated. The Council of 381, attended by at least four bishops from Cyprus, voted that in the future laymen should not be permitted to participate in the election of church dignitaries. Priestly control was strengthened. The poor were eliminated from having any control in a religion that had started with little pomp and ceremony. The church assumed all political power as well.

The separation of the Eastern and Western churches, once ruled as a unit from Rome, was made official in 395. However, a division already had occurred during the reign of Constantine. Constantine established his capital in the east at Byzantium, which was named Constantinople (present-day Istanbul, Turkey) in his honor. Cyprus fell under the jurisdiction of Constantinople.

For some time the *patriarchs*, "bishops," of Antioch (in what is now Turkey), the capital of the Eastern diocese, had claimed the right to consecrate the archbishop of Cyprus. In Pope Innocent's time, Alexander, patriarch of Antioch, complained that the Cypriots were consecrating their own bishops. The pope ordered submission, but the Cypriots argued their case at an important church council. Archbishop Anthemius, the most powerful church leader of Cyprus at the time, told of a vision he had had. In the vision the apostle Barnabas directed his words and actions in defense of the Cypriot claim for independence. The powerful patriarch of Antioch argued forcefully that the small Cypriot church belonged in his jurisdiction. The final decision confirmed the independence of the Church of Cyprus. It was ranked equally with the churches of Antioch, Jerusalem, Alexandria, and Constantinople.

This was an important decision for the future. With the power of the church went the power of authority within the island.

THE BYZANTINE EMPIRE

The Byzantine Empire was a continuation of the Greek heritage. Geographic and trade patterns linked the island of Cyprus more closely with Greece than it ever had been with Rome. During the more than eight centuries of Byzantine rule, the culture of Byzantium penetrated every aspect of Cypriot life.

Except for religious disputes, this was a time of peace in Cyprus. But peace came at the price of privileges for those who worked the land. The ruling class consisted of wealthy landowners. Laws were strict. Farmers who owned no land became *serfs*, ''slaves'' or ''servants,'' and were forbidden to leave the land on which they were born. The church itself became a wealthy landlord.

The separation of church and state was weak at best. Byzantium was a theocracy. The emperor invested the patriarch of Constantinople and the patriarch crowned the emperor *eleo Theou*, ''by the grace of God.'' Yet there were times when the church pleaded the case of the common man. It was the only hope for those who lived a life of poverty.

The island also became known as a place of banishment for undesirable political rivals from the mainland. Thousands of prisoners were sent here and were immediately put to work for the benefit of the ruling class. While peace may have seemed a desirable benefit to some, the unfair practices that brought it about were soon to brew discontent that would lead to revolution.

MUSLIM RELIGION

In the reign of the Roman Emperor Heraclius came the rise of another world religion. Abdulqasim Muhammad ibn Abdullah ibn al-Muttalib ibn Hashim, known to the world simply as Muhammad, had visions from God. Muhammad felt the words of God, or Allah, were aimed at his people, who had become sinful. Allah said there was no need for churches or synagogues, no need for priests or magi. Anyone could talk to God through prayer.

The religion Muhammad founded is called Islam and its followers are called Muslims. There are five pillars, or basic beliefs, of Islam. A Muslim must profess faith in God by saying: "There is no God but God (Allah), and Muhammad is his Prophet." The faithful must pray five times a day, give to charity, fast from dawn until sunset during the month of Ramadan, and make a pilgrimage to Mecca (the holy city in Saudi Arabia) once in a lifetime. Conversions to Islam swept from Arabia east through Persia and west over the provinces of the Byzantine Empire.

In 639, an Arab named Mu'awiya became *emir*, "prince," of Syria, a land east of Cyprus on the Mediterranean Coast. To start his journey to power, Mu'awiya planned a massive naval engagement against Cyprus. Using the newly captured base at Alexandria in Egypt, also on the Mediterranean Sea, he fitted out a fleet of seventeen hundred ships. Mu'awiya landed in Cyprus in 648. He attacked the city of Constantia, located at the site of the ancient city of Salamis. Constantia, founded by the Romans during the fourth century A.D., was one of the wealthiest Cypriot cities at the time. Most of the people were killed. Legend says that the articles stolen from Constantia alone filled seventy ships.

Mu'awiya imposed an annual payment of seventy-two hundred gold pieces. When the Cypriots failed to pay the tribute, another force was sent to mete out punishment. By the year 688 the Cypriots were burdened with debts to both the Arabs and to the

Richard the Lionhearted (left) and a castle built by the Knights Templar

imperial Byzantine treasury, which had been imposing heavy taxes.

The raids by Mu'awiya were only the first of a series of attacks against Cyprus. Many were quick attacks by pirates, others were well-planned campaigns by Muslims against their Christian enemies. It was not until the end of the tenth century that the Byzantine forces drove the Arabs out of Cyprus.

THREE CENTURIES OF WAR WITH THE ARABS

During the three centuries of war with the Arabs, many cities and towns were destroyed, never to be rebuilt, but new cities began to appear.

In the twelfth century Isaac Comnenos, a Byzantine governor, set himself up as the king of Cyprus and defended his right to the title until defeated by the king of England, Richard I, called Richard the Lionhearted.

While on a crusade to the Middle East to capture the Holy Lands from Muslim nonbelievers, King Richard's ships were wrecked off the southern coast of Cyprus. The wrecked ships were plundered by forces of Comnenos. Richard took time out from his crusade to capture Cyprus for England. The newly conquered territory proved to be a troublesome conquest. The Cypriots unsuccessfully tried to rid themselves of the intruders. To remain in control Richard would have had to garrison many of his troops on the island. He did not have that many men to spare if he were going to complete his goal in the Holy Land, but he still had no intention of giving the Cypriots their freedom. Instead he turned over the governing chore to a French monastic order called the Knights Templars. Their payment would be whatever they could plunder from the land itself.

The Knights Templars, in turn, found it hard to govern the island. They relinquished control to Guy de Lusignan, who maintained his own troops although being technically in the service of King Richard. Lusignan lived only two years after assuming control of Cyprus in 1192, but the dynasty he founded ruled the island as an independent kingdom for more than three centuries. Officials of the Roman Catholic church attempted to take over the Eastern Orthodox church of Cyprus, collecting all tithes of the church and forcing Cypriots to use the Latin order of the mass. Although the Church of Rome officially claimed dominance, Cypriots refused to accept the Western form of Christianity.

In the meantime Egyptian Muslims had systematically captured Christian fortresses along the eastern shores of the Mediterranean. Many fleeing the Muslim presence came to Cyprus. As the only remaining Christian base against the Muslims, the island prospered, and its kings gained importance. However, native Cypriots still were regarded as little better than serfs.

The Turks used this fort in the harbor at Paphos for their defense.

THE OTTOMAN EMPIRE RULES

Two Italian republics, Genoa and Venice, became interested in the base at Cyprus. For a while the port of Famagusta was ceded to Genoa, but through intrigue and financial power Venice soon took over the rule of the entire island. Not many changes occurred. Venetian governors proved corrupt and tyrannical. During the short Venetian reign the Turks attacked the island, taking plunder and captives, who were sold into slavery.

In the summer of 1570 the Turks led a full-scale invasion of Cyprus. They landed near Larnaca. Within three weeks Nicosia, the capital, fell and was destroyed. Twenty thousand Nicosians were put to death, and every church and public building was leveled. Only one city, Famagusta, put up a defense, but it was unsuccessful. Cyprus became part of the Ottoman Empire and remained under Turkish control for the next three hundred years.

The former leaders of Cyprus who did not manage to escape were killed. The few Greek Orthodox Christians who survived faced new rulers. The conquerors abolished the feudal system and allowed peasants to work their own farms. Another action that resulted in long-range change was the granting of land to Turkish soldiers who had taken part in the campaign. They became the nucleus of the island's present-day Turkish minority.

The Turks were more lenient in their acceptance of the Church of Cyprus. In ruling their extended empire, the *sultans* (Muslim religious and secular rulers) often found it convenient to use the existing governing organization of a territory to collect taxes and to enforce the laws of the land. In their own country there was no division between the leaders of the Muslim faith and the political rulers. In Cyprus, as they did throughout their empire, the Ottomans turned to the Greek Orthodox church to administer affairs of state. Thus they gave the Cypriots a taste of autonomy, while still remaining in control of laws and taxes.

The military strength of the Ottomans declined gradually after the sixteenth century. The rulers were often dishonest. Various Cypriots attempted to gain greater power over their own government. Attempts were made to redistribute the country's wealth, but because there was little wealth left, reforms failed.

There were periodic uprisings against Turkish rule because of the high taxes levied on the population. However, Greek Cypriots were not strong enough to overthrow their oppressors. One nearly successful attempt was made, but the results were disastrous. Archbishop Kyprianos was accused of plotting rebellion. He and hundreds of priests and important laymen were arrested and put to death on July 9, 1821. It was many years before the church was able to regain its original power.

Chapter 4
BRITAIN ASSUMES
CONTROL

BRITISH COLONIAL RULE

In 1821 Greek nationalists revolted against the Ottoman Empire. With the help of Great Britain, France, and Russia, Greece gained independence when the fighting ended in 1829.

Great Britain was drawn into the Crimean War with Russia in 1854. Both France and Great Britain were afraid that if Russia took land from Turkey, Russia would become too powerful. It was already evident that the Ottoman Empire was weak. A war was fought in the Crimea (a peninsula south of Ukraine in the Black Sea).

Twenty years later there were more rebellions in the Ottoman-held Balkan region (the peninsula in the southeast of Europe that is bordered by the Adriatic and Ionian seas on the west and the Black and Aegean seas on the east). Local Christians were demanding reforms in territorial government. When Turkey failed to give up total control of all laws and the policing force, Russia took up arms under the pretext of protecting the Slavic populations of the Balkans. The Turks were forced to sign a treaty giving virtual control of the Dardanelles (the strait that connects the Sea of Marmara with the Aegean Sea) to Russia. European nations refused to acknowledge the treaty.

Benjamin Disraeli fostered secret negotiations between Great Britain and the Ottoman Empire.

Great Britain, under the direction of Prime Minister Benjamin Disraeli, held secret negotiations with the Ottoman Empire. The outcome was that Cyprus was to be administered by Great Britain, and Great Britain in turn would back up the Ottoman army if there were any other aggressive military moves by Russia. The terms of this secret covenant provided that an annual fixed payment would be paid by Britain to Ottoman Turkey. In that way Turks could assert that they had not surrendered Cyprus to the British, but had merely turned over the government to Great Britain.

This annual tribute became a great source of dispute and future negotiation. The Cypriots found themselves not only paying the tribute in taxes but they also were charged with the expenses incurred by the British colonial administration. To make matters even worse, the tribute was never even paid to Ottoman Turkey. It

Winston Churchill was British undersecretary of state for the colonies in 1907.

was deposited in the Bank of England to pay off Turkish Crimean War loans. The people of Cyprus therefore felt that they were being forced to pay a debt that was not theirs.

The tribute was finally reduced, but not abolished, through the efforts of the British undersecretary of state for the colonies, Winston Churchill, in 1907.

At the onset of World War I the Ottoman Empire joined forces with the Central Powers, which included Germany, Austria-Hungary, and Bulgaria, against Britain. Britain at once annulled the treaty that had been so painstakingly drawn up and annexed Cyprus for herself. Cyprus was used by the British during World War I as a naval base. In 1915 Britain offered the island to Greece as a bribe if Greece would enter the war on the side of the Allies. King Constantine of Greece refused the offer, declaring neutrality.

It was not until the Treaty of Lausanne in 1924 that Cyprus officially became a crown colony of the British Empire. The change meant very little to the average Cypriot. Greek Cypriots were still arguing for *enosis*, "union," a merger of the island's government with mainland Greece. The revised constitution for the Colony of Cyprus did not, as many Cypriots had hoped, change the Turkish debt charge. When the debt charge was finally dropped after considerable pressure, other fees were substituted to cover "imperial defense."

Taxes were again raised to meet economic deficits brought on by the Great Depression. Mob violence erupted in October 1931. "Enosis, now and forever" was the rallying cry. Before the uprising was stopped, six people had died, scores had been injured, and some two thousand jailed.

Britain responded by putting the country under military rule and abolishing the constitution. Press censorship was instituted, and several of the leaders in the rioting were exiled. Municipal elections were suspended, and until 1943 all officials were appointed by the governor who became a dictator, empowered to rule by decree.

The measures seemed particularly harsh, considering that they were applied to the Turkish community as well. Turkish Cypriots had not taken part in the riots of 1931, because they did not wish to be part of Greece. The teaching of both Greek and Turkish history was forbidden. The display of flags of either ethnic group was not permitted. Gatherings of more than five people required official permission. The Cypriot Orthodox church was subjected to government investigation, which caused even more hard feelings. Even the election of an archbishop required the governor's approval.

Before the outbreak of World War II, Cypriots worried about the expansionist plans of Benito Mussolini, the Italian dictator.

The harsh rules imposed on the country forced the enosis movement underground. Much of the fiery oratory and headlines came from London, from those Cypriots who had fled oppression. The British government refused to recognize that such sentiments for unification with Greece were held by the majority.

Instead of again offering the island to Greece, the British went about establishing local governments that they thought could be handled more easily. The pattern of splitting governing bodies into small geographical units had long been practiced under the Ottoman Empire. The *mukhtan,* "village leader," and *aza,* "elected elder," were important figures. The British seemed to feel that giving responsibility at the village level would satisfy those who wanted to make decisions on a higher level. This was not true.

WORLD WAR II

Cypriots of all religious beliefs were worried over the expanding power of the Italian dictator, Benito Mussolini, and the

Roman Catholics. When World War II broke out, with Italy allied with the Axis powers of Germany and Japan, the Cypriots supported Great Britain, particularly after the Axis powers invaded Greece in 1940. More than thirty thousand Cypriots fought under British command during World War II. Although Cyprus was important as a supply base, the island escaped military action. Most Greek Cypriots thought that as soon as the war was over their union with Greece would come about. They felt that they had earned it.

During the war Britain made no move to restore the constitution that had been abandoned in 1931. However, permission was granted by the governor to form political parties. One of the first groups to take advantage of this was the Communist party, which founded the *Anorthotikon Komma Ergazomenou Laou*, "Progressive Party of the Working People," (AKEL). It came about quite naturally following the wartime alliance with the Soviet Union, but it alarmed the church and merchant groups. A loose federation of Nationalists backed by the church and those working for enosis formed their own *Panagrotiki Enosis Kyprou*, "Panagrarian Union of Cyprus." (PEK).

In the municipal elections of 1943, the first that had been allowed since the crackdown in 1931, AKEL gained control of the important cities of Famagusta and Limassol. Both Communists and conservatives backed enosis, but they clashed on almost all other issues.

Late in 1946, after the end of World War II, the British government announced plans to liberalize its colonial rule of

Cyprus. Delegations of both parties were invited to sit in on the discussions. The British also allowed the return of the leaders who had been exiled in 1931, and the strict religious laws that had been imposed were repealed.

Instead of being pleased by the turn of events, Greek Cypriots were angry that there had been no mention of enosis. In October 1947 the bishop of Kyrenia was elected as head of the Cypriot church. As Archbishop Makarios II, he opposed any policy that did not actively promote union with Greece.

The assembly met simply as a consultative body, and twenty-two Greek Cypriots refused to attend unless enosis was the only matter on the agenda. However, eighteen members were present. Of these, seven were Turkish Cypriots, two were nonparty affiliated Greek Cypriots, one was a Maronite from the small minority of non-Orthodox Christians, and eight were members of the Communist AKEL group. The eight left-wing members proposed setting up a full-scale self-governing state, which did not agree with the opposition's demand for enosis. When their proposals were ignored, they joined with the others in fighting the British mandate. With the assembly deadlocked, matters came to a standstill.

Meanwhile the Church of Cyprus strengthened its control of the community. Bishop Makarios became both the spiritual and secular leader of the country. His major accomplishment was the planning of a plebiscite (vote by the people) that resulted in a 96 percent favorable vote for enosis in January 1950. However, in June 1950 Archbishop Makarios II died.

Kykko Monastery,
where Makarios studied,
is the most famous
monastery in Cyprus.

Chapter 5

A STRUGGLE
FOR POWER

THE CHURCH

In October 1950 the bishop of Kition was elected to succeed the deceased head of the church. He took office as Makarios III. At age thirty-seven, he became the youngest archbishop in the history of the Church of Cyprus. He pledged not to rest until union with "Mother Greece" had been achieved.

The new leader of church and state had been born Michael Christodoulos Mouskos to peasant parents in the village of Pano Panayia. The date of his birth was August 11, 1913. Makarios always felt that the number thirteen was a lucky number for him. His father was a shepherd. As a young boy Makarios spent much of his life in a small hut beside a sheepfold. Although his family was poor, as were many around him, he had friends and relatives who gave him moral support.

Makarios became drawn to religion early. On finishing elementary school in 1926 he entered the Kykko Monastery as a novice. He was then thirteen. The church gave him a fine education. Yet without money, travel was an extravagance. He was eighteen before he saw the sea that surrounded his homeland.

In his youth Makarios refused to grow a beard, which had been ordered by his abbot, and was almost expelled because of it. He was an independent student with ideas of his own. In 1938 he was ordained deacon and sent to the University of Athens on a scholarship. Because of the German occupation of Greece during World War II he was unable to return to Cyprus immediately. He stayed on to study law and came to love the city of Athens.

After the war, on January 13, 1946, Makarios was ordained a priest. Some months later he won another scholarship offered by the World Council of Churches and set sail for the Methodist Theological College at the University of Boston. For most of the time between his twenty-fifth and thirty-fifth years he was out of Cyprus. Travel and study abroad gave Makarios a much broader, more sophisticated view of the world. Over the years he studied oratory and became adept at swaying an audience with his dynamic speaking style. While still a student in Boston he made one trip home, and during this time he gave a number of sermons that impressed those who heard him. A few months before his final exams Makarios was elected bishop. He almost refused the honor, because he had set his sights on becoming a professor at the University of Athens. He was persuaded that it was his duty to accept and he never regretted the decision. It was not long before he was elected archbishop by representatives of 97 percent of the Greek Cypriots. His popularity was at its height.

Makarios was active from the beginning in promoting the

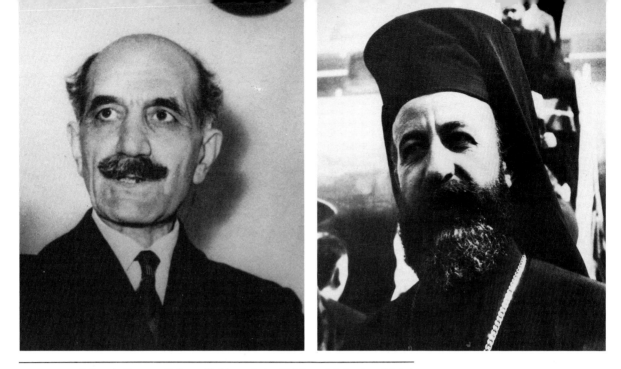

Colonel George Grivas (left) and Archbishop Makarios (right)

enosis cause. He did not neglect to seek support from left-wingers as well as conservatives. He saw that the anticolonial feeling among the newly independent states could be turned to his advantage. An unofficial Greek-Cypriot delegation had already gone to the United Nations to present the result of the January enosis plebiscite. It was in 1951 that Makarios III made his first appearance before this international body.

THE MILITARY

It was also in 1951 that Makarios met Colonel George Grivas, who was becoming known for his strong feelings on the subject of Greek union. Grivas was born in 1898 in the village of Trikomo about thirty-one miles (fifty kilometers) northeast of Nicosia. He was a good student, and after the end of his elementary education at age seventeen, he was sent to Athens to enter the Greek Military Academy. He served in the military during the Greco-Turkish War of 1920 to 1922. When the Italians invaded Greece in 1940, Grivas was a lieutenant colonel assigned as chief of staff to an infantry division.

During the Nazi occupation of Greece in World War II, Grivas led a right-wing organization in guerrilla warfare. He was a man of extremes. Although he had earned a reputation for bravery, he often used underhanded methods. Grivas resented having to share leadership with Makarios. But if both were to see a union with Greece, each needed the other. Makarios preferred to settle issues with diplomacy. Grivas was ready to fight.

In August 1954 Greece's United Nations representative officially requested that the subject of self-determination be put on the agenda of the General Assembly's next session. The British continued to feel that it was an internal issue, not one for international negotiation. Turkey, of course, entirely rejected the idea of union with Greece. The Turks felt that they had never given up possession of Cyprus. They felt the British had tricked them out of their rightful ownership.

Eighteen percent of Cypriots were not Greek. They were a minority with a different language, religion, and set of traditions. The attitude of the Cyprus Turkish Minority Association was that in the advent of British withdrawal, control of Cyprus should revert to Turkey, ignoring the fact that Turkey had given up all rights to the island in the 1924 Treaty of Lausanne.

An underground political organization known as *Volkan*, "volcano," spawned the *Turk Mukavemet Teskilati*, "Turkish Resistance Organization," (TMT) a guerrilla group that fought—at least with propaganda—the idea of union with Greece. Yet the TMT generally kept clear of any direct action because under British rule the Turkish minority status and identity were protected.

The British Institute in Nicosia was set on fire during demonstrations in 1955.

By the fall of 1954, rioting had become commonplace among the Greek Cypriots. It soon became a question of when a British military force would be sent to keep peace. The local police force was too small to handle the situation.

The British colonial government announced that they would punish advocates of enosis with up to five years in prison. Archbishop Makarios ignored the threats. Anti-British feelings were further heightened when Britain made an agreement with Egypt to evacuate British forces from the Suez Canal zone in Egypt and set up headquarters for British Middle East land and air forces in Cyprus. Meanwhile Colonel Grivas had returned to Cyprus to conduct secret talks with Makarios.

In December the United Nations, with Britain sitting in as a permanent member of the Security Council, turned down a proposal to discuss the Cyprus problem. The reaction in Cyprus was immediate and violent. A general strike was called. Even schoolchildren demonstrated in the streets. It was the worst rioting since 1931.

Negotiation had failed. Now it was time for Grivas to put force behind his words. The *Ethniki Organosis Kyprion Agoniston,* "National Organization of Cypriot Fighters," (EOKA) was formed. What it desperately needed were military supplies.

On the night of January 25, 1955, a small ship loaded with dynamite hugged the deserted south shore of the island. They did not know they were being watched until suddenly the trap was sprung. A British destroyer aimed its searchlights across the water, and a landing party was ready to seize the cargo.

It was a blow to the EOKA cause, but it only delayed the first strikes by two months. A series of well-coordinated acts of violence were aimed at the police and government installations in Nicosia, Famagusta, Larnaca, and Limassol. The main link of communication, the radio station in the nation's capital, was blown up.

National attention was now focused on Cyprus. Everyone agreed it was no longer a local affair that could be easily settled. A meeting, known as the Tripartite Conference, was held in London in August. Representatives from Greece and Turkey were invited, but no Cypriots were asked to attend. The meeting broke up in September, having accomplished nothing. However, a bomb was set off at the Turkish consulate in Greece, which brought about rioting and hand-to-hand fighting between Turks and Greeks in the main cities of Turkey.

Shortly after the disappointing Tripartite Conference, British Field Marshal John Harding was named governor of Cyprus. He came with a plan that offered British cash for modernization and development throughout the island on acceptance of limited self-government and a postponement of any vote to determine whether enosis would become a reality. He was there, he assured

44

Left: British Field Marshal John Harding became governor of Cyprus in 1955. Above: Greek Cypriots celebrate after hearing Makarios would be returning to Cyprus.

them, to maintain law and order. Grivas told the governor that halfway measures would not be accepted.

Official talks were held between Makarios and Harding in January 1956, but each side accused the other of negotiating in bad faith. Shortly afterward Makarios was arrested and charged with rebellious activities. The bishop of Kyrenia and two other priests joined him in prison and were eventually exiled to the Seychelles, a group of islands off the coast of Africa. This only infuriated Greek Cypriots and put more power into the hands of the militant Grivas. After two years Makarios was allowed to return. Grivas was eventually forced to leave with the understanding that his guerrilla fighters would not be punished.

Other officials from Great Britain were sent to negotiate terms. Harding was replaced by Governor Hugh Foot, who proposed a five-year cooling-off period that would be followed by a vote of

In 1959, Archbishop Makarios (on the left) returned to Cyprus from exile.

"self-determination," allowing Cypriots to decide for themselves the course of action to be taken. Both Greece and Turkey disliked the terms.

Next came the Macmillan Plan, which suggested that there be two separate legislative bodies. This form of partition was rejected. Finally serious talks were conducted for the first time suggesting an independent Cyprus, with neither enosis nor partition. The general feeling was that compromise was the only road to peace, and a conference was called in London to draw up the basis for a constitution. Those who gave up the goal of unification with Greece were equally afraid that partitioning their country into Greek and Turkish communities would only cause more civil war. Independence seemed the only course, but it was not the course hoped for by the majority of Cypriots.

Chapter 6
AN INDEPENDENT
COUNTRY

INDEPENDENCE

The Republic of Cyprus came into being on August 16, 1960.
The constitution called for a government divided into executive,
legislative, and judicial branches. Great pains had been taken to
give the Turkish minority a voice in the governing process. The
constitution stipulated that there be a Greek Cypriot president and
a Turkish Cypriot vice-president, each elected by his own people.
Other small minority groups were given the option of joining
either ethnic group. The Armenians, Maronites, and Roman
Catholic Cypriots chose to be identified as Greek.

The Supreme Constitutional Court was composed of three
judges, a Greek Cypriot, a Turkish Cypriot, and a neutral
representative with no ties to either Turkey or Greece who was to
serve as president of the court. Other safeguards for the Turkish
minority specified in the constitution provided that the two
groups be represented in the country's public service employment
base on a 70 percent to 30 percent ratio. The army, to be composed
of two thousand troops, was to consist of 60 percent Greek
Cypriots and 40 percent Turkish Cypriots.

During the first general election for the House of Representatives, of the thirty-five seats allotted to Greek Cypriots, thirty were won by supporters of Makarios and five by the AKEL. The fifteen Turkish seats were won by supporters of the newly elected vice-president, Fazil Kucuk.

Independence did not bring peace to the new government. The rise of Turkish nationalism, which had not been overly strong during British colonial rule, came to the fore now. Turkish Cypriots attempted to win more rights from the majority party. There were frequent stalemates in the legislative process between the Greek Cypriots and the Turkish Cypriots because each side had veto power.

On November 30, 1963, President Makarios proposed adding thirteen amendments to the constitution. These amendments were intended to make the governing process more efficient. Any changes had to be approved by Britain, Greece, and Turkey, who had participated in the original drafting of the constitution. These three countries had agreed to help keep the peace and to offer economic assistance until the government of Cyprus was well established.

Some of the proposed amendments were to change the ratio of public service jobs to more closely follow the actual population ratio, which would have benefited the Greek Cypriots; to abolish separate voting by Greek Cypriots and Turkish Cypriots for the passing of certain laws; to abolish the separate administration of justice; to cancel the right of veto power by either the president or vice-president; and to abolish separate municipalities and establish unified ones.

Turkish Cypriot leader Dr. Kucuk apparently agreed to consider the proposals, but the Turkish government on the mainland saw it

Above: Greek Cypriots aim their weapons at a Turkish Cypriot stronghold. Left: A British soldier looks at the bodies of two dead Turkish Cypriots.

as a weakening of Turkish influence in the area. No agreement was reached.

The atmosphere remained tense. On December 21, 1963, violence erupted in Nicosia. Two Turkish Cypriots were killed during a riot. Underground organizations of both groups started open warfare. EOKA members renewed their cry for enosis, and the TMT demanded partition. The problem started in Nicosia as a minor skirmish but spread to other towns and finally covered the entire island.

Actual warfare lasted for several months. Everyday life was interrupted and the business of government was shut down. The United Nations Security Council finally sent in a peacekeeping force, while Turkey threatened to invade the island to protect its own people. On one occasion the Turkish fleet was just a few miles offshore and turned back only after President Lyndon B. Johnson of the United States delivered a threat to Turkey that it would jeopardize its own security if force were used in Cyprus.

Turkey was afraid of Russian aggression on its borders at the time. It could not afford to alienate its only strong supporter, the United States, against such aggression. Turkey did not land its troops, but the Turkish forces did bomb the northern coastline of the island, causing the destruction of several villages and scores of casualties.

When peace was finally restored with the aid of United Nations forces, the balance of power between the two communities was drastically affected. After three years of conflict within the legislative body, Vice-President Kucuk set about organizing the Turkish Cypriots. In the past there had been no geographical boundaries between the two groups. Turks lived next to Greeks, and differences were tolerated.

Throughout 1964 a total of between twenty thousand and twenty-five thousand Turkish Cypriots pulled up stakes and poured into towns and rural areas where their ethnic group predominated. The Turkish Cypriot members of Parliament and the government withdrew into the Turkish quarters of Nicosia and the other major towns. The machinery of government was turned over to the Greek Cypriots by default. The Turkish Cypriots, in turn, installed in Nicosia their own administration, police, courts, and an army trained and led by mainland Turks.

After the fighting ended the Turkish Cypriots were in control of no more than 5 percent of the island's territory, but they were well organized and equipped. The Greek Cypriots were willing to tear down the barricades that separated the two sides, and they expected the Turkish Cypriots to do likewise. The Turkish Cypriots, however, refused to let Greek Cypriots enter their enclaves unless they signed pledges recognizing the provisional Turkish Cypriot administration. Few Greek Cypriots were willing

Eventually the Turkish flag flew over parts of Nicosia and the Cathedral of Saint Sofia became a mosque.

to do so, fearing it would imply they recognized this upstart state within a state.

There seemed to be no compromise. The gulf between the groups widened. Actually the Turks were harming themselves economically. Most of the developments in business, tourism, construction, and agriculture took place in the area controlled by the Greek-backed government.

Turkish flags continued to fly over their enclaves. Shipments of supplies from mainland Turkey helped the Turkish Cypriots hold out against a virtual siege. Barbed wire and guard posts separated these Turkish Cypriots from the rest of the country. The enclaves varied in size from a collection of villages with a close-knit family organization to the Turkish Cypriot quarter of Kyrenia, which was a walled city.

Those who came to the nation's capital crowded into the Turkish quarter, which had no adequate housing. Tents and hastily constructed shacks were all that was provided. Slum conditions resulted. Most of these refugees had given up their land and houses for the security of a Turkish Cypriot settlement. With only Greek Cypriot representation the governing body of the Republic of Cyprus had no authority within the enclaves. All it could do was wall off the refugees and not permit them to leave. Not until 1968 was this changed.

United Nations forces were again sent to keep order. Under pressure, some restrictions were relaxed. Greek Cypriots, for example, furnished water, electricity, and telephone service to the Turkish enclave in Nicosia. Some jobs, such as seasonal agricultural work, were offered to Turkish Cypriots, but their leaders discouraged such a practice. Young Turkish Cypriots living within their walled compounds found themselves growing up no longer able to speak the language of their neighbors.

Business continued to be conducted within the legislature, but Turkish Cypriots refused to acknowledge any acts or laws passed without their approval. By the close of 1967 Turkish Cypriots had set up their own administration to govern their people. The fifteen former Turkish Cypriot members of the House of Representatives joined other members who had held office under the original constitution. They functioned as an executive council to carry out the affairs of the Turkish community. President Makarios described the council as illegal. He said any actions by that body would be declared null and void.

DISSENSION WITHIN THE GREEK COMMUNITY

President Makarios had problems within his own party as well. Polykarpos Georkajis, who had been appointed minister of the interior, was a hard-core member of the EOKA. A military dictatorship was established in Greece after three Greek colonels staged a coup on April 21, 1967. The coup leader, George Papadopoulos, had made himself prime minister of Greece by force. In 1969 Papadopoulos charged that Georkajis had been involved in an assassination attempt against his life. The prime minister insisted that Makarios arrest Georkajis and turn him over to Greek military officers.

Georkajis was popular in Cyprus, and Makarios hesitated to carry out the orders. However, shortly after the demand was made public Georkajis was found murdered in his automobile. His murderers were never caught. Makarios was blamed for not protecting his former cabinet member.

In the summer of 1971 violence increased. Colonel Grivas, who was living abroad, called Makarios a traitor in an Athens newspaper. Soon Grivas returned secretly to Cyprus to rebuild his guerrilla organization, EOKA B. He again campaigned for enosis with plans for eventually overthrowing the Makarios regime.

In March 1972 the bishops of Kition, Kyrenia, and Paphos joined the anti-Makarios forces to demand that Makarios give up his position as president as well as relinquish his religious title of archbishop. Makarios confronted the challenge by inviting the Orthodox patriarchs of Alexandria, Antioch, Constantinople, and Jerusalem to meet as the Supreme Synod to consider his case. He was judged innocent of all charges and retained his power.

Grivas was becoming an embarrassment to the Greek government through his use of brute terrorism. However, he was popular in conservative circles in both Greece and Cyprus. Few wanted to oppose him. The problem was solved on January 24, 1974, when the general died of a heart attack.

However, right-wing forces continued to try to overthrow Makarios by force. In Greece, Papadopoulos and his supporters had been overthrown in November 1973 by Colonel Ioannides. The new Greek prime minister wanted Makarios overthrown. Makarios narrowly escaped death in an attack by the Greek-led Cypriot National Guard. The guns of ten Soviet-made T-34 tanks pounded the Presidential Palace to rubble. Makarios escaped to the British military base on Cyprus, and from there to Malta. Eventually he was flown to London.

The National Guard proclaimed Nicos Sampson president, but it was evident that the orders were coming from Athens. Sampson had once been a terrorist working for the EOKA. He was hated by Turkish Cypriots. He reportedly had led murder squads into Turkish areas.

Turkey sent envoys to London to ask for British help in negotiating a treaty. Many European countries condemned the brutality of the Athens military regime and its involvement in Cyprus, and demanded that Makarios be returned to power.

The United States took no action to support the Makarios government, but Secretary of State Henry Kissinger sent Undersecretary of State Joseph J. Sisco to London to stave off an expected Turkish invasion.

The Turks demanded the removal of Sampson. They also sought to remove Greek officers of the National Guard, who were exerting more power than they were supposed to have by constitutional mandate.

Even as Sisco tried to negotiate terms between the two sides, Turkish ships were already on their way to a landing on Cyprus shores. Last-minute concessions might have stopped the invasion, but by July 20, 1974, the Turkish army was in Cyprus.

Turkish supplies being unloaded at the port of Kyrenia

Chapter 7

A COUNTRY DIVIDED

TURKISH INTERVENTION

This war was not a short-lived local skirmish that would soon be forgotten. Claims were made that at least 200,000 Greek Cypriots were left homeless and expelled to the south in the first wave of occupation. At least 3,000 Greek Cypriots disappeared into mainland Turkish jails, and their property was looted and sent back to Turkey.

Several human rights organizations tried to investigate charges that the Turks had been abusive. Although some of the allegations were substantiated, nothing was done about it. Furthermore Turkish Cypriots argued that these reports had not covered alleged abuses by Greek Cypriots from 1963 to 1964 when Turkish Cypriots were forced to flee to Turkish settlements, leaving their homes behind.

President Makarios returned in December 1974 to take over leadership of the Greek community from acting president Glafkos Clerides. Five months earlier, the Greek military regime of Ioannides had collapsed under the pressures caused by the invasion of Cyprus. At that time, a democratic government led by

Rauf Denktash (left) became head of the Turkish Federated State of Cyprus and Archbishop Makarios (right) continued leading the internationally recognized Republic of Cyprus.

Constantinos Karamanlis took power in Greece. For all practical purposes Cyprus was divided into two political entities. The partition was upheld by Turkish military strength concentrated in the north of the island, while the government of the Republic of Cyprus, composed entirely of Greek Cypriots, claimed authority over the entire island.

On February 13, 1975, the Turkish Cypriot leader, Rauf Denktash, proclaimed the existence of the Turkish Federated State of Cyprus. The Turkish lira was adopted as legal currency. However, the Turkish Cypriot representative to the United Nations stated that the new regime was not seeking recognition as an independent state. He claimed that the action was taken to safeguard the security of Turkish Cypriot citizens.

Both in Athens, the capital of Greece, and Nicosia partition was denounced. President Makarios spoke out sharply against the action, saying that splitting the country would result only in economic disaster. Upon his death in the summer of 1977 from a

Archbishop Chrysostomos speaks with Britain's archbishop of Canterbury.

heart attack at age sixty-three, there seemed to be no one who commanded the power or the trust of the people enough to take over the task of bringing peace. However, Spyros Kyprianou, head of the Democratic party, ran and won on a platform that promised to continue the struggle against the Turkish occupation forces.

After Makarios's death, the positions of president and head of the church were split between Spyros Kyprianou as president of the Republic and Archbishop Chrysostomos as head of the Church of Cyprus. It was Chrysostomos, however, who pleaded the case of the Greek Cypriots in Washington and at the United Nations. United States President Jimmy Carter and United Nations Secretary General Kurt Waldheim listened but offered no solution.

In 1983 the Turkish Cypriot community declared itself a separate state, the Turkish Republic of Northern Cyprus, but it remains recognized only by Turkey. Turkish Cypriot leader Rauf Denktash states that one of the preconditions for any kind of peaceful solution is for Greek Cypriots to recognize his community as a political equal. What he is demanding is a unified, bizonal state, sharing power in a federal structure with unrestricted movement and property rights. What causes much debate is that any solution must give mainland Turkey the right to intervene to defend Turkish Cypriots.

Turkish-occupied area

Nicosia

*United Nations forces
have been trying
to keep peace
between the Greek
and Turkish factions
since 1964.*

On the other hand, the Greek Cypriots demand that the Turks hand back to the Greek community substantial amounts of territory and property taken in 1974 and that Greek Cypriots be allowed to return to the homes they had once occupied in the north. They also demand that the Turks remove their thirty thousand troops from the island.

Turkey has gradually withdrawn some of its troops, but it has been estimated that approximately twenty-five thousand still remain. The country remains cut in half by a United Nations patrolled line, the "Green Line" that separates 170,000 Turkish Cypriots in the north from almost 650,000 Greek Cypriots in the south and runs through the middle of the capital of Nicosia.

For a long time Greek Cypriots refused to have anything to do with a peace-finding conference, feeling that any such negotiations would admit recognition of the Turkish independent state. Some concessions have been made that allow a controlled movement of visitors from one sector to the other, but both sides disagree on the number of Greek Cypriots that should be allowed to return to the north.

The Turkish sector is having a harder time surviving alone than the Greek, although Turkish Cypriots occupy some of the best farmlands in Cyprus. Turkish Cypriots have been cut off from international trade and international lending institutions. Their combined income is about one-third that of Greek Cypriots. They depend heavily on subsidies from Ankara. Turkey would like to become a member of the European Community with trade sanctions, but the conflict gives the Greeks a pretext for blocking membership.

The Socialist party of Greece has been criticizing conservative Prime Minister Constantin Mitsotakis for accepting the idea of a conference, claiming that Greece is being dragged into meetings that would be harmful to its national interests.

President Kyprianou continues to try to solve his country's problems within the framework of the United Nations, although the AKEL party appeals directly to the workers in the north, advocating economic cooperation as a way to improve conditions for the whole country. Kyprianou will not hear of any talks that would legitimize the results of the Turkish intervention.

The fight for enosis has been abandoned. The Greek Cypriots who were in the forefront of that campaign realize that if enosis came about, Turkish Cypriots would be seen to have a right to rebel. Most Greek Cypriots now advocate a pro-Western policy that would encourage the United States to pressure Turkey into making concessions. The United States sees Turkey as a strong military ally with advantageous ties to Central Asia. It would take a diplomatic juggling act to satisfy all parties concerned.

On July 18, 1991, President George Bush arrived in Cyprus at the invitation of Greek Prime Minister Mitsotakis. This was the first visit by an American president since a visit by President Dwight Eisenhower in 1959.

Mitsotakis was still hopeful that after seventeen years a settlement could be reached. "We have just gone through the Gulf War, and the attention of the world, and particularly the United States, is toward this part of the world," he said. "The war was waged by all to protect the international order and carry out the United Nations decisions. Now is the time for these principles to be applied to Cyprus."

Now that the Berlin Wall has crumbled and Germany has been reunited, there is hope that the sandbags and barbed wire that run through the capital city of Nicosia can be rolled away. The main problems are how much land will be returned to Greek Cypriots who were forced out of the occupied zone by Turkish troops and what form of government will be acceptable to both sides.

It will be impossible for the two ethnic groups of Cyprus to discard their national identities and begin establishing a hybrid Cypriot ethnic identity. However, both need to discard those elements of their cultures that foster prejudice and violence.

A policy of cultural pluralism must be supported by a political and social system founded on justice, a system that will serve the interests of the Cypriot people, not the interests of foreign powers.

Chapter 8

LIFE-STYLES

Cyprus is a small country, but it is hard to generalize when describing what life is like on the island. There are differences between the two dominant ethnic groups. Language and culture set them apart. Another dividing factor is the contrast between the life-styles of those living in the rural areas and those who have come to the larger cities. But one thing is certain, a strong family structure is recognized throughout the island.

Cyprus is still a male-dominated world. Only the most modern thinking families, who have probably been educated abroad, favor equal career opportunities for both sons and daughters. Large families are still the custom, and women are respected for child rearing and home management, whether they are of Turkish or Greek descent.

The *kaphenion*, "coffee shop," society is composed of Greek men who are found sitting in or in front of the local coffee shop watching the world go by. Serious political discussions may take place or the sitters may just contemplate in solitude. Coffee, wine,

Men gathered outside a kaphenion

and a limited menu of food are usually offered, but no one is hurried. A whole day may be spent at one small table with friends and neighbors. Card playing and backgammon are common pastimes. On weekdays, the kaphenia are populated by male retirees. Women have their own habits of visiting, but usually their meetings are in homes.

Family outings are often picnics in the countryside. On special days, such as a religious holiday or a birthday, a more elaborate feast is prepared. It is called a *klephtiko*. A fire is lit inside one of the beehive clay ovens in the open air. When the flame dies down, the embers are covered with green leaves to dampen the fire and supply moisture. The meat, mutton or goat, is placed on top of the leaves and the oven is sealed for a period of some hours until the meal is done. The meat is then eaten with bread and a vegetable

A wedding procession in a small village

salad. Beer and brandy are served. Wine is more popular for everyday use.

Many traditions have grown up around the village wedding ceremony in Greek communities. Everyone in the town is invited. The celebration often lasts for two or three days. Many small points of protocol must be observed, such as the ceremony of filling the mattress, the blessing of the bride by her father, and the ceremonious shaving of the groom.

Within the Greek Orthodox church the duties of the best man and bridesmaid are spelled out in detail. Following the ceremony they are expected to give financial assistance and even physical protection in times of crisis. They may later become godparents of the couple's first child, thereby entering into a virtual blood relationship, because their children are legally prohibited from marrying their godchildren.

The groom receives gifts at the wedding celebration.

On the day of the wedding, guests are invited into the new home immediately following the ceremony. After giving their presents to the newlyweds, the best man pours each a glass of brandy and offers a piece of traditional seed cake. Then the feasting really begins. There is usually a band composed of accordion, violin, and drums. The young couple starts the dancing, and during this time paper money is pinned to their clothes until the clothes are completely covered.

Within Turkish Cypriot communities, much of the wedding tradition is dictated by the presiding Muslim teacher of the village. In prominent families a *mullah*, or local religious leader of high rank, may make the trip from the mainland to be on hand for the final blessing.

RELIGION

In a country where religion plays such a predominant role in both communities, the Communists are the only organized force

A Cypriot Greek Orthodox church and clergy

proposing secular solutions to social problems. They have not
been strong enough to overthrow the power of the Cypriot Greek
Orthodox church. There was a time when British administrators
weakened the church's position. They took away its right to
collect taxes and its right to appoint teachers in the schools, but
Greek Cypriots still turn to their bishops for leadership.

The position of Islam in the Turkish Cypriot community differs
from that of Greek Orthodoxy. The Church of Cyprus was
identified with Greek nationalism and the campaign for enosis.
Within the Turkish community religion was not used for political
leverage, but its laws and customs are directly dictated by the
rules of the Sunni branch of Islam.

The Islamic faith is built around the teachings of the prophet
Muhammad. Many holy men from other religions are considered
disciples and teachers of the true faith. Thus many prophets of the
Judaic Old Testament and Jesus himself are given a place in the
Muslim scheme of things. The word *Muslim* means "one who has
surrendered himself to God's will." Daily prayers are called from

Saint Sofia has been transformed into a mosque on the outside by adding minarets, and on the inside by removing Christian symbols and adding an Islamic decor.

the minaret of the mosque five times a day. There are strict laws of dress and approved food that may be followed.

Evkaf Idarest, ''Turkish Religious Trust,'' usually called Evkaf, is the prime representative of the Turkish Cypriot community. During the colonial period the Evkaf functioned as a government department. Evkaf's revenues are derived from its large land holdings and other property placed in trust for religious purposes. However, Evkaf estimates it has lost 54 percent of farmland and 98 percent of its buildings as a result of the 1974 administration partition.

The spiritual leader of Turkish Cypriots is the *mufti* of Cyprus. Over the years there have been many changes in the role of the mufti. His role today is essentially as a judge rather than an administrator.

The importance of religion in the politics of Greece and Turkey has had an impact on the role of religion in Cypriot politics. The

Greek Orthodox church remains a major force in Greek politics. Institutional Islam has a lesser role to play in Turkey. However, it is the foundation of Turkish Cypriot home life. All these different traditions deepen the rift between the two ethnic groups both in Cyprus and on the mainland.

LANGUAGE

The country is further divided by language. Three major languages were used in Cyprus in the late 1970s, Greek, Turkish, and English.

Greek, in Cyprus as in Greece, has three idioms. The formal liturgy of the Orthodox church is *koine*. It has not changed over the centuries. The most important form of Greek today is *demotiki*. It is the standardized language spoken throughout the Greek Cypriot community. It is what is taught in schools. But there is a third form, *katharevousa*. It is the result of eliminating all borrowed forms and colloquial expressions to re-create an elegant modern Greek style evoking the classical Greek literary idiom.

In the 1970s Turkish was the first language of one-fifth of all Cypriots, the entire Muslim population. It is very similar to what is spoken on the mainland. But by 1979 the Turkish national language institute made sweeping changes. It tried to eliminate ''loan words'' from other languages and to replace them with roots found among the Turkish nomads of the central Asian steppe. A Latin alphabet was introduced to replace Arabic script.

In spite of the fact that there was strong anti-British feeling at the time of independence, English is used as the second language by most Cypriots. It became important during the period when Cyprus was becoming increasingly internationalized and

Schoolchildren (left) and a student at the Hotel and Catering Institute (right)

interested in world trade. It has become the language that Greek Cypriots and Turkish Cypriots use to communicate with each other.

EDUCATION

Although Cyprus has no university, the educational level of its citizens is very high. A great deal has happened within the twentieth century to improve the situation. In the early days of Turkish rule, only one school existed in Cyprus. It was not until the twentieth century that the educational system was helped by the Greek Orthodox church, and even within the rural areas classes were taught by the elders of the communities who were fortunate enough to be able to read and write.

During British rule, education was a priority, although secondary education was available only on a limited basis. After the formation of the Republic of Cyprus, education became the

The Cyprus Forestry College

responsibility of a new ministry of education. However, this ministry represented the interests of the Greek population exclusively.

Elementary education is provided free of charge. It is compulsory for the six years between six and twelve years of age. Secondary or high school education is voluntary, but almost 80 percent of all pupils still are able to continue, paying a small amount of money each year in fees and other expenses.

Secondary education follows the same general pattern in Cyprus as in Greece. It is divided into two cycles of three years each. The first offers a general education and the second a more specialized course of study. In addition to the Greek state schools, there are a number of private establishments, mainly teaching courses in foreign languages.

There are several technical and vocational schools, including the Forestry College, the Hotel and Catering Institute, and the School for Nursing and Midwifery.

Within the Turkish community most of the formal classes for older students are managed by Muslim leaders.

HEALTH

The climate and a tradition of cleanliness have made Cyprus one of the healthiest places in the world, but this was not always the case. There were swampy areas that harbored the malaria-carrying anopheles mosquito. Many a crusader died in Cyprus on his way to the Holy Land. It has only been within the twentieth century, with great help from the International Health Division of the Rockefeller Foundation, that swamps were drained and malaria controlled.

Veterinary services have now controlled a dangerous disease carried by stray dogs. The dogs were not necessarily rabid, but they carried an infection that was passed on to humans through scratches or bites. Pest control teams have gone to work on the scourge of locusts that often demolished crops in the past.

In 1960 all the major urban centers had hospitals or clinics staffed by British, French, and Greek-trained physicians. Because Cyprus is a relatively small island, everyone is within traveling distance of some health facility.

There is a marked difference in the quality of health care between the two sectors of the country since separation. In the Turkish sector matters have been worsening because of the lack of public funds. Existing hospitals and clinics in the north are understaffed. The prices of medical supplies have escalated. Problems with water sources are great and sanitation systems are inadequate.

In the Greek Cypriot sector government budgets for health and

The Hospital Archbishop Makarios in Nicosia

welfare programs are substantial. There are no shortages of professional care givers, and private funds seem to be able to entice competent doctors to practice in Cyprus.

The Turkish Federated State of Cyprus is not internationally recognized as an independent state; therefore, specialized agencies that might help, staffed by the United Nations and the World Health Organization, are unavailable. All relief funds from the United States, the European Economic Council, and the Greek Orthodox church are funneled into the southern sector.

SPORTS

Cyprus has a strong athletic tradition going back to the time of the early Greeks. Well-preserved ancient gymnasiums have been discovered. Cypriot gymnasts are reported to have participated in the original Olympic games.

During the Turkish occupation, athletics were not greatly

Horseback riding (left)
and game bird hunting (above)

emphasized, although challenges of weight lifters were often sources of exciting competitions between rival villages.

Under British tutelage, physical education became part of the school curriculum. The most popular national sport is soccer. The Cyprus Football (soccer) Association oversees the thirty-six teams in the three league divisions. Cyprus has taken part in World Cup matches.

Individual sports such as tennis and horseback riding are popular, and of course there are water sports such as sailing, scuba diving, and water skiing, which are enjoyed mostly by tourists. For a few patient souls, snow skiing is available on Mount Olympus a few weeks every year.

Game shooting became such a popular pastime that the government had to limit the amount of birds any one hunter could bring in for fear of permanently wiping out certain species.

There is little fresh water for fishing, and what catches are made in the sea surrounding the island are taken by professional fishermen.

Folk singers and dancers in the national costume

THE ARTS

The most important and popular forms of art in Cyprus are music and dance. The structure and form of music have changed little over the centuries. In its purest form music is played on the *aulos*, a shepherd's flute. For performances a violin and *bouzouki*, a stringed guitarlike instrument, are added. Certain melodies have been retained in the ancient Greek style.

Dances are now performed generally only on special occasions, such as weddings, by pairs of men and by pairs of women. The men's dances are more lively, some being traced back to ancient origins. The dance of the knife is probably derived from an ancient war dance.

Dancing at a wedding reception

Poetry is something that everyone enjoys and that nearly everyone at some time or another has tried to compose. There are competitions at many of the annual fairs. These *chatismata*, attended by hundreds of people for hours on end, consist of a dialogue in rhyming couplets between two contestants. Some can be composed for the sake of poking fun at people or events. Others can be serious in mood. Of course, not all have literary merit, but many would-be poets print their own copies and sell them on street corners for a few coins.

Marketing longer written works is more difficult. The Cypriot dialect is sufficiently different from the spoken and written language of the Greek mainland to prevent acceptance elsewhere.

Most of the visual art of the country has been created for

A production of the classical Greek play Andromache *by Euripides*

religious purposes, although a few Cypriot artists have exhibited their work abroad. In the Turkish sector, art is demonstrated in fine crafts similar to the brass and leather work found in mainland Turkey.

In 1971 a theater company was organized to present classical and modern plays in Greek.

Perhaps the main reason an independent art of Cyprus has not developed is due to its lack of resources and its cultural dependence on the Greek and Turkish mainlands. While fine craft industries of a traditional nature have flourished in the island for most of its history, only in recent years has there been a market for art in the larger urban centers of the island.

A panoramic view of the village of Kakopetria in the Troodos Massif

Chapter 9

URBAN CENTERS

CITIES

   Although much of the economic growth of the island is taking place in the cities, more than half the population of Cyprus lives in villages of less than five hundred people. In general villages were located near an ample supply of water where the land was rich for agriculture. Families congregated together for protection and for sociability. Settlements were almost always built around a village square, the center of everyday life, surrounded by coffee shops, themselves the main meeting places, together with the church or mosque, the school, and other public buildings.

   Cyprus, in common with all countries throughout the world, is experiencing a movement of the population from the country to the towns. The migration has not been overwhelming, however, simply because many wage earners prefer to commute from their home villages to their city jobs. Few people can afford to buy or rent dwellings in the main urban centers. Commuting has the added advantage of allowing people to live in their own villages with their families, supplementing their income with their small farms.

This rural house was built of stone and then covered with plaster.

For those who have remained on the land, cash incomes are approximately half those in urban areas, but farmers are still adopting urban behavior patterns. The influence of the towns is thus spreading outward. The old custom of planned marriages, for instance, is now in the process of disappearing. Suburban-style buildings, symbolic of the wealth and education of the owners, are being erected in all villages. Villagers go to the nearest town for shopping, for entertainment, and for higher educational opportunities. No one remains as isolated as in the past.

ARCHITECTURE

Apart from churches and mosques, there are few buildings more than a hundred years old. In part it is because of the impermanence of the materials used (adobe brick in the plains) and because the stone used in more durable buildings was simply confiscated for use in newer construction.

*In the mountains, igneous rocks are broken
into blocks to be used in construction.*

Rural architectural styles have stayed virtually unchanged since
early times. Homes are designed for people who spend their lives
in the open air and need only minimal shelter for themselves and
their animals. In the lowland areas houses are usually built of
sun-dried mud bricks covered with a thin coating of plaster. In the
Troodos Mountains area, the igneous rocks are broken into large
blocks for building purposes. In other places softer limestone and
sandstone may be used. Although materials differ from one
district to another, the construction of the house follows a more or
less consistent pattern.

Floors are of packed dirt, brick, mosaics of pebbles, or in more
prosperous homes, slabs of local golden marble. The ceiling is
usually supported by arches of timber or stone. The roof is
generally of earth resting on reeds or a wattle of woven sticks. In
the lowland areas, the roof is flat so that it can be used for the
drying of agricultural produce and for sleeping outdoors during
the hot summer months.

In rural areas, cooking is done in a beehive-shaped clay oven, which is separate from the house.

The house usually consists of three rooms, one for eating and sleeping, one for storage, and one for animals. The house is usually built around a courtyard where there might be a well, a beehive-shaped clay oven, and an outdoor toilet.

The new buildings that are being built close to the larger towns are one or two-story, single-family dwellings without accommodations for livestock. Each stands a regulation ten feet (three meters) away from its neighbors. Usually painted in attractive pastel colors, the houses are frequently unfinished, with plans for additions as the family grows.

The dowry system, still a part of the traditional way of life on the island, dictates that the father of the bride provide a house for the newlyweds. All the members of the family contribute toward payment for the house as part of their duty, and those who are handy with construction may assist in the actual process

A modern house in Nicosia

of building. If the family is unable to purchase land for such a home, an addition to the family home has to suffice.

The government has built only a handful of subsidized houses, which are sold to the occupants on a rent-purchase plan for those in the lowest income groups.

The Turkish administration constructed a number of apartments and houses for the refugees after the intervention, but these are substandard and poorly built. Within the cities, high-rise buildings are becoming increasingly common, but most are used for office space, not for living quarters. A few wealthy Cypriots have built lovely villas of Mediterranean style near the towns. A second vacation home, either in the mountains or at the ocean, also may be part of the family plan. But this is the exception to a life-style that, although distinctly better than Third-World poverty, is not known for its opulence.

The beach at Larnaca

LARNACA

Until recently Larnaca was a small, sleepy old town with a
population of less than twenty thousand. However, it has grown
in importance with the opening of its international airport some
three miles (five kilometers) south of the city. The airport was
entirely reconstructed to accommodate commercial jets after the
Turkish takeover of most of Nicosia. Larnaca is situated on the
southern shore of Cyprus. The town is of special interest because
of the fine museum that contains many excellent archaeological
artifacts from the adjacent site of Kition.

Larnaca was settled in the earliest years of Cyprus's history and
later grew in importance when it was dominated by the
Phoenicians. The port was used as the main shipping center for
the export of copper from the mines of Tamassus, twenty-five
miles (forty kilometers) to the northwest.

Today chapters of its history can be traced through several
centuries of buildings. The old Turkish fort built in 1625 was once

A fort (below) built by the Turks in 1625 and a quiet street (inset) in Larnaca

The Djami *(Mosque) Kebir (above) and the church of Ayios Lazaros (inset)*

used as a prison and a military barracks, but it has now been converted into a museum. Close by is the domed *Djami* (Mosque) Kebir in what was until recently the Turkish Cypriot quarter of town.

Perhaps the most famous building is the church of Ayios Lazaros. According to legend, Lazarus, who was resurrected from the dead by Christ, was expelled from Jerusalem by the Jews and sailed to Kition. Here he died and was buried. In 890 his tomb was discovered, but his remains were taken to Constantinople and later to France. Nevertheless, the original burial site has been consecrated with a church built in the ninth century. It has been restored several times since.

Wooden catwalks have been built over the diggings at Kition to allow visitors to see the excavations. A limestone statue of the Greek god Zeus (right), from about 500 B.C., found at Kition

Kition, which today is considered almost a suburb of Larnaca, has been a treasure trove for archaeologists. Wooden catwalks have been built over some of the diggings to give visitors an idea of the extent of the early building. Already, early Mycenaean pottery (from the twelfth century B.C.), alabaster vessels, gold jewelry, scarabs from Egypt, carved ivory, and a superb enameled drinking vessel in the shape of a horn decorated with hunting scenes have been recovered and are on display in the museum.

Many chamber tombs were discovered in the courtyards of the houses. A complete copper workshop was uncovered along with what appears to be a bathing complex similar to what has been found in Greek ruins on the mainland.

Nicosia, the capital,
lies almost in the
center of Cyprus.
A newer section
of the city (above)
and the municipal pool (left)

A wall built by the Venetians in the sixteenth century still stands in Nicosia.

NICOSIA

Nicosia is the capital of the Republic of Cyprus. It lies at 536 feet (163 meters) above sea level in the center of the Mesaoria plain with views of both the Kyrenia range and the Troodos Massif edging its horizons. It contains few buildings of outstanding interest, but its trees and colorful shrubs soften the landscape.

The old section of the town was fortified by the Venetians with strongly built walls of stone that had been plundered from eighty churches and other buildings as well as from monasteries and cemeteries. The walls enclose a complete circle with eleven bastions and projecting towers, which were each given the name of a Venetian officer in charge of their defense. At the same time, all the buildings outside the walls were destroyed and razed so as to leave a clear line of fire from inside the city. Cannons were a newly invented weapon to be dealt with.

The fast-growing city is at present divided by the so-called

Left: A view from the old section of Nicosia shows the modern section and new buildings under construction.
Right: Eleftheria Square is in the center of the capital.

United Nations Green Line, separating the Greek Cypriots from the Turkish Cypriots and the military forces of the mainland.

Although there is evidence that the earliest occupation of the site was in 300 B.C., the most important ruins come from the time of the Crusades. Some hundred Templars took refuge in a Byzantine castle during a local uprising. It occurred on Easter Sunday 1192. Later the castle was made into a military fort. This, in turn, was replaced by a more extensive walled château, monastery, and citadel.

Nicosia has withstood more than war. It has been severely damaged by earthquakes several times and suffered a raging fire in 1857. Its population was decimated by a serious epidemic of cholera in 1835.

*Scenes of Nicosia, clockwise from left, are:
a market in the narrow streets of the
old city, the Archbishop's Palace,
and the Folk Art Museum.*

In 1964 the Greek and Turkish sectors of the city were separated
by the United Nations Green Line in an effort to keep the peace.
But in 1974 Turkish mainland forces stormed the city from the
northwest, and the city was divided between the Republic and the
Occupied Zone with only one crossing point permitted
immediately west of the old town walls. During this time many of
the more valuable items displayed at the Cyprus Museum were
temporarily transferred to Athens for safekeeping, something
Turkish Cypriots strongly resent. There is also a folk art museum
with interesting examples of embroidery and clothing, carved
furniture, and agricultural implements from the past.

The industrial port at Limassol

LIMASSOL

There is a lot of good-natured rivalry between the towns of Nicosia and Limassol, the second-largest town on the island. Each claims to be the more prosperous and the more beautiful. The one fact that cannot be disputed is that Limassol almost doubled in size near the end of the twentieth century. Its spectacular growth was caused largely by the transplanting of Greek Cypriot refugees from the Turkish-held territory.

The town has a comparatively short history. It rose to importance in the Middle Ages as a trading center. It still serves as a busy industrial port. It is known for its plants that process wines, spirits, beers, and soft drinks, for it is the nearest port to the vineyards. It is also an important export center for agricultural and mining products.

Although there are tombs from about 1300 B.C. in the area, Limassol's main claim to fame is that it was a Crusader base when it was attacked by the Saracen Muslims in the 1200s. Today the harbor is dotted by large loading booms for maritime shipping.

Above: The Medieval Museum of Cyprus is in Limassol Castle.
Below: This market in Limassol sells produce grown in
the fertile soil of the area.

The Monastery of St. Heracleidos (courtyard above) in Tamassus is named after the first Greek Orthodox bishop of Cyprus. A new home in Tamassus (inset)

TAMASSUS

Tamassus has long been famous for its seemingly inexhaustible supply of copper. Its mineral wealth was first discovered around 2500 B.C. The mines were mentioned in the Homeric epic the *Odyssey*. It was a Phoenician colony in 800 B.C. Later the city and the mines were given by Alexander the Great to King Pnytagoras of Salamis as a reward for the assistance of that Cypriot king in the capture of Tyre.

The town was the earliest center of Christianity in Cyprus, and one of its earliest bishops, Abbot Nilos of the Makheras Monastery, eventually became archbishop. Past this monastery there is a beautiful winding drive through the wooded foothills of the Troodos Massif.

An asbestos mine in Pano Amiandos in the Troodos Massif

PANO AMIANDOS

Farther into the mountains is the small village of Pano Amiandos where the hillside has been terraced by giant machinery that claws away at the dirt to reach the asbestos deposits. The quarries are located above the winter snowline and are usually worked only from April to September. Asbestos has been mined here since 1907.

TROODOS

There is a town called Troodos at an elevation of 5,659 feet (1,725 meters). It is the highest continually inhabited place in Cyprus, being both a summer and a winter resort. Before modern refrigeration, snow was brought down from the mountains to help preserve food in the valley.

The colorful fishing boats and nets of Paphos harbor

PAPHOS

Paphos is now the name generally given to the twin towns of
Ktima, the upper and newer part, and Nea Paphos, which
contains the main archaeological sites nearer the harbor. It is the
most westerly port in Cyprus. It was developed as a commercial
base and as a shipbuilding center. As with almost all towns on the
island, it has a long history and was probably first settled by
adventurers from Lebanon and Syria as early as 1180 B.C.

There are ruins from all the most important periods of Cypriot
history, including the temple of Aphrodite. A new type of rock-
cut tomb in Alexandrian style from the Hellenistic period appears

Above: Tombs of the Kings, built in the fourth century B.C. in
Paphos, contain underground tombs carved from solid rock. No kings
were buried here.   Above right: A theater built of limestone
blocks from the second century A.D. is in use today.

in nearby Nea Paphos. These tombs, misleadingly named "Tombs
of the Kings" because of their opulence, must have belonged to
wealthy Paphians or high government officials. They were also
used during the Roman period and later by Christians. There is
also a large Greek amphitheater, and the pillar to which the
town's Roman governor bound St. Paul. Catacombs and a number
of well-preserved churches remain from the Byzantine period.

In later years the harbor was clogged with silt and almost
abandoned. However it was dredged and reopened at the turn of
the century.

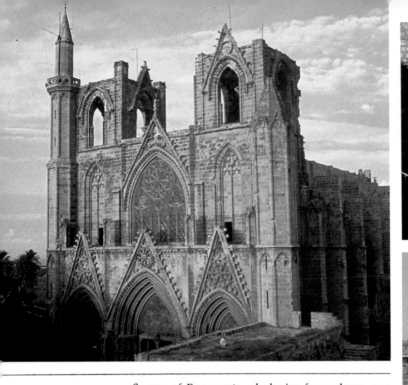

*Scenes of Famagusta, clockwise from above, are:
the French Gothic St. Nicholas Cathedral
with a minaret added to one of the
bell towers, an old narrow street,
and a wall built in the fifteenth century.*

FAMAGUSTA

Famagusta, which means "hidden in the sand," is a city of two
completely separate quarters, the medieval walled city, occupied
by Turkish Cypriots, and the Greek Cypriot "suburb" of Varosha.
The city was once known for its wealth and extravagance, but
many of its fine buildings were destroyed in a battle with the
Turks in 1571.

The central point of old Famagusta is the magnificent Latin
Cathedral of St. Nicholas, consecrated in 1326. It was later
converted to use as the Lala Mustapha Mosque. The new town is
in direct contrast as a tourist seafront coastal resort. Orange
groves thrive and add to the beauty of the district.

The harbor of Kyrenia

KYRENIA

It has been said that Kyrenia is the most picturesque of all Cyprus towns. It was founded in the tenth century B.C., but did not develop into a politically important city-state until it was fortified by Byzantium. It is the only one of the principal towns that is not a market center for the region, because it is only ten miles (sixteen kilometers) from the nation's capital.

The Museum of Kyrenia houses an extraordinarily well-preserved—now meticulously restored—classical Greek commercial vessel recovered from the bottom of the sea in the early 1970s.

A shepherd leads his flock across the Mesaoria plain (top).
A man carries his basket of lemons (left) and
women harvest potatoes (above)—two important crops.

Chapter 10

THE COUNTRY'S FUTURE

AGRICULTURE

In spite of a great deal of promotion of the manufacturing sector, Cyprus still remains predominantly an agricultural country. Three categories of land ownership exist: private, state, and communal. In 1973 the largest private landowner was the Church of Cyprus. The second-largest owner was the Turkish Religious Trust, known as Evkaf. Unrestricted ownership of private land dated only from 1946, when the British administration changed the land code that had been in effect since the time of the Ottomans. Communal tracts were once set aside as common grazing land for a whole community.

Most farms are small. This poses problems in soil conservation and irrigation. Some families found their plots of land scattered from one village to another as rights of inheritance divided land for the heirs. Marriages outside the immediate village further cut parcels into difficult-to-manage sections. The agricultural cooperative movement in Cyprus was begun in 1909, but was not

Olives (left) and grapes (right) grow well in Cyprus

used to its full advantage until the founding of the Cooperative Central Bank. The bank's initial function was to furnish societies with funds for short-term loans to members.

A large number of crops have been grown successfully on the island, especially wheat, barley, market vegetables, melons, fruit, nuts, and hay for forage. Oranges, lemons, grapefruit, and tangerines proved to be valuable export crops as a more efficient system of irrigation was developed. At the time of partition, water sources were frequently blocked and new pipelines and ditches had to be dug on both sides of the Green Line. Olive oil is also a valuable export.

Local wineries receive their crops from the terraced hillsides and valleys in the Troodos Mountains. Vegetables in great variety

A goatherd in the fields

are cultivated for home consumption, including such common ones as cabbage, cauliflower, carrots, cucumbers, onions, potatoes, squash, and tomatoes, as well as artichokes, asparagus, okra, and taro.

Poultry and goats make up the largest category of livestock. Hogs are now raised, although during the time of Muslim domination, pork was a forbidden item on the menu.

FORESTRY

The state has been trying to replant some of the deforested areas of the island. Replanting is a problem aggravated by the fact that 90 percent of fuel used for cooking and heating is wood. Even fast-growing softwoods are cut before they mature, because of the crucial need for the product.

Pine trees have been planted to help stop erosion.

Control measures have been set up restricting the free pasturing of goats in forestlands. Acacia and eucalyptus were introduced in the lowlands to halt erosion, and about 385 square miles (1,000 square kilometers) have been planted with commercially valuable pine.

FISHING

Fishing has been of minor importance throughout Cyprus's recorded history. In the water surrounding the island there is a general deficiency of nutrients that are essential to the growth of a large marine population. Local fishermen can barely supply the demands of local villages.

A gypsum mine

MINING

Copper, the island's most valuable mineral, has been an important asset since prehistoric times, but today the supply has almost been exhausted. Other economically important minerals are chromite, iron pyrite (mined for its sulfur content), asbestos, gypsum, and umber, a pigment used in paint.

INDUSTRY

At the time of independence the manufacturing sector consisted almost entirely of small family-owned businesses employing

Small industries produce such items as margarine (left)
and sugar wafers (right), which are called biscuits in Cyprus.

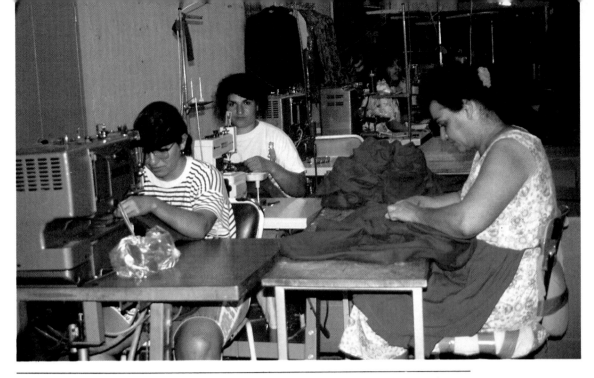

Apparel is an important export. Seamstresses at work in a clothing factory

fewer than five workers. An increase in production never seemed practical because of a limited domestic market, the generally low level of income, and the shortage of skilled labor. Cypriot buyers of high-priced quality items preferred imported goods.

To stimulate industrial development, the government has reduced or abolished import duties on raw materials. Taxes also were almost eliminated on new industries. Training centers for management and technical personnel, as well as for laborers, were set up.

Industry was left to private enterprise. The government made direct investment only in the petroleum refinery at Larnaca. During the first ten years of independence, some seventy manufacturing plants were constructed. Particularly in Nicosia and Limassol plant structures were built for lease to promising small industries. These included biscuit and margarine plants, fruit and meat canning plants, a brewery, paper products factories, textile and hosiery mills, pharmaceutical plants, and metal fabricating factories. Yet as a whole the output remained geared to the local market. The exception was the export of canned goods.

When Turkey cut the country in two, about one-third of the manufacturing sector was under Turkish control. However, the Turkish Cypriots cut off their main market by setting up blockades between the two ethnic communities. To the south in the Greek Cypriot territory, they too had problems. Certain raw materials, of which the north had been the major supplier, were no longer available.

The sharp drop in incomes in the south after mid-1974 forced the manufacturing sector to look for ways to export its produce. The First Emergency Economic Action Plan, proposed in 1975-1976, attempted to develop such labor-intensive industries as clothing and footwear aimed for export markets. Efforts were made to help reestablish Greek Cypriot entrepreneurs who had fled the Turkish Cypriot zone. Frequently they had packed up what few belongings they could carry with them, leaving their modest businesses behind. To make it possible for those who had fled to rebuild, the government sought to lend money at very low interest rates to those who wanted to make a fresh start to help restore the marketing and manufacturing structure they had left behind.

The government hoped to encourage foreign investors by guaranteeing up to 75 percent of the loans made by commercial banks for industrial products. All of these efforts resulted in the tripling of exports of manufactured goods.

In the Turkish sector progress was slower. There was a shortage of qualified technicians and skilled workers. Yet the economy was bolstered by the continued help sent from mainland Turkey.

Getting ready to pour cement at a construction site in Nicosia

CONSTRUCTION

Cyprus is experiencing a building boom caused partly by the redistribution of its population following the Turkish intervention. Permanent housing must be provided for the hundreds of refugees who poured into the cities in the south.

Turkey too had to provide for the large number of immigrants who were settling in the Turkish sector. Additional barracks also were needed for the military force that took up residence in the north.

In spite of internal conflicts, Cyprus is trying to rebuild its tourist industry. New hotels are being built. Cyprus has always been a favorite spot for European vacationers because of its proximity to other nations' capitals and because of its geography and climate. Its mild Mediterranean seasons, sweeping beaches,

A modern resort area near Famagusta (right) and ruins from an ancient castle at Paphos from the Byzantine Empire (above), which was destroyed by an earthquake in 1222. These are only two of the many tourist attractions in Cyprus.

mountains, and historical landmarks are bringing tourists back to Cyprus. And they will continue to come as long as the government can guarantee protection against civil conflict.

New brick-making factories have opened in the Greek sector to replace northern sources for materials. There is still a shortage of skilled workers, in part caused by the exodus of talent to other countries following the civil war, but tradesmen are being imported. There is very little unemployment within the country.

As the economy has grown and become more diverse, so has the island's economic stability, highlighted by low inflation and near full employment.

To attract Western businesses, it is important that Cyprus operate much like other Western industrial democracies with a government, judicial system, and accounting methods based on a system of free enterprise.

THE LAW

In this small island there is little serious crime. Burglaries are infrequent. Of the six thousand to eight thousand people found guilty in the courts each year, two-thirds are responsible for only minor traffic violations. There are no trials by jury, for it would be next to impossible to find an unbiased jury with no family or other ties to the accused person.

The island's courts have the right to inflict four types of punishment on offenders: death, imprisonment, flogging, and fining. Flogging has not been used since the establishment of the republic, and the death sentence has not been imposed since 1962.

The Cypriot judicial system is composed of a mixture of constitutional law, common law based on Ottoman and English precedent, and public law. In addition there are five main religious groups (Greek Orthodox, Muslim, Armenian, Maronite, and Roman Catholic) that have total jurisdiction over the matters of marriage, divorce, and other family relations of members of their churches.

MODERNIZATION

Cyprus has done a remarkable job of keeping pace with its changing economy. Its automatic telecommunications service is ranked among the best in the world. With three satellite earth stations and three submarine cable systems, the island has direct dial service to more than 120 nations.

The transportation system is similarly well developed. Cyprus has two international airports in Larnaca and Paphos, 30 miles (48 kilometers) and 100 miles (161 kilometers) from the capital,

The highway connecting Nicosia and Limassol

Nicosia. They serve as connecting links with carriers from Europe and the Middle East.

The highway network connects all towns and most villages. At the time of Turkish intervention, Cyprus had one of the largest number of licensed vehicles of any developing country in the eastern Mediterranean area. These roads have been kept in comparatively good repair because of dependence on truck and bus transportation, as well as private cars. The only railroad in the country is a private narrow-gauge line that carries ores from inland mines to loading facilities on the coast.

A young Nicosian girl and a man from Kythrea preparing kabobs, *pieces of marinated meat grilled with vegetables on a skewer*

THE FUTURE

Cyprus has the foundations for a peaceful future if long-standing hostilities can be put to rest. It has been said that both Turkish Cypriots and Greek Cypriots are refugees from their ancestral homes. Both are suffering economic woes as a result of the island's partition. While the international community is focusing its attention on the diplomatic resolution of the Israeli-Palestinian conflict, there is little attention paid to the Greek Cypriot-Turkish Cypriot conflict. Perhaps the mutual desire for a better life will bring about a durable political system based on communal cooperation rather than on rivalry and conflict.

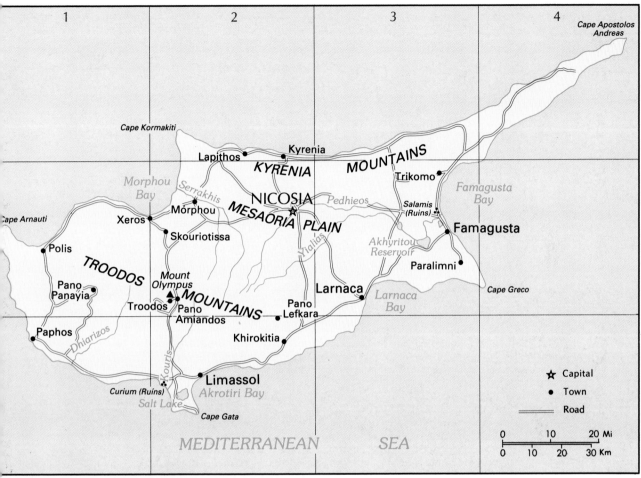

```
          1                    2                    3                    4
                                                              Cape Apostolos
                                                                   Andreas




           Cape Kormakiti
                                      Kyrenia
                Lapithos •    KYRENIA     MOUNTAINS
                                                 • Trikomo
    Morphou                                                   Famagusta
      Bay            Serrakhis   NICOSIA    Pedhieos           Bay
                       Morphou  MESAORIA  PLAIN      Salamis
Cape Arnauti    Xeros •                              (Ruins) •
                        • Skouriotissa                         • Famagusta
    • Polis                                   Akhyritou
                                              Reservoir
           TROODOS       Mount                              • Paralimni
      Pano •          Olympus                 Larnaca
      Panayia          ▲ MOUNTAINS                    Cape Greco
              Troodos  Pano       Pano •    Larnaca
                       Amiandos   Lefkara    Bay
    • Paphos   Dhiarizos
                                • Khirokitia
                     Kouris
                               • Limassol           ☆  Capital
         Curium (Ruins)    Akrotiri Bay             •  Town
              Salt Lake                            ═══  Road
                   Cape Gata
                                               0        10      20 Mi
         MEDITERRANEAN          SEA            0    10   20    30 Km
```

tography by: University of Kentucky Cart Lab.

MAP KEY

			Pano Lefkara	C2
		Kouris (river)	C2	Pano Panayia	B1
		Kyrenia Mountains	B2, B3, A3	Paphos	C1
Akhyritou Reservoir	B3	Kyrenia	A2	Paralimni	B3
Akrotiri Bay	C2	Lapithos	A2	Pedhieos (river)	B3
Apostolos Andreas, Cape	A4	Larnaca	B3	Polis	B1
Arnauti, Cape	B1	Larnaca Bay	B3	Salamis (Ruins)	B3
Curium (Ruins)	C2	Limassol	C2	Salt Lake	C2
Dhiarizos (river)	C1	Mediterranean Sea	C1, C2, C3	Serrakhis (river)	B2
Famagusta	B3	Mesaoria Plain	B2, B3	Skouriotissa	B2
Famagusta Bay	B3	Morphou	B2	Trikomo	B3
Gata, Cape	C2	Morphou Bay	B1, B2	Troodos	B2
Greco, Cape	B4	Mount Olympus	B2	Troodos Mountains (Massif)	B1, B2
Khirokitia	C2	Nicosia	B2	Xeros	B1
Kormakiti, Cape	A2	Pano Amiandos	B2	Yialias (river)	B2, B3

MINI-FACTS AT A GLANCE

GENERAL INFORMATION

Official Name: Republic of Cyprus (*Kipriaki Dimokratia*, Greek; *Kibris Cumhuriyeti*, Turkish)

Capital: Nicosia. The capital city is divided into Greek and Turkish sectors; the Turkish sector has been renamed Lefkosa by the Turks.

Government: Two states actually currently exist in Cyprus. Since 1974 the northern one-third of the island has been under the control of the Turkish Cypriots. In February 1975 the Turkish Cypriots formally constituted a Turkish Federated State of Cyprus (TFSC), which proclaimed independence as the Turkish Republic of Northern Cyprus (TRNC) November 15, 1983, and is recognized only by Turkey. The southern two-thirds, the Greek Cypriot zone, is controlled by the government of the Republic of Cyprus, still the internationally recognized government of the whole island. The Green Line, controlled by the United Nations' peacekeeping troops, separates the two regions and divides Nicosia. Both communities have their own presidents, council of ministers, legislature, and judicial system.
　According to the August 16, 1960 constitution, the government is divided into executive, legislative, and judicial branches. It is a unitary multiparty parliamentary democracy with a unicameral legislature. The president, a Greek Cypriot, is the head of state and government and the vice-president is a Turkish Cypriot. Each is elected by his own people for a 5-year term. The highest court of justice is the Supreme Constitutional Court. The constitution provides for safeguards for the Turkish minority, and division of power in the government between the Greek and Turkish Cypriots in proportion to their numbers.

Religion: Greek Orthodox and Islam are the two major religions. Some 77 percent of the people are Greek-speaking Orthodox Christians and some 18 percent are Turkish-speaking Muslims. The rest of the population consists of Armenians, Maronites, Roman Catholics, and other minorities. The Greek Cypriot church is identified with Greek nationalism and the church remains a major force in Greek politics. In the Turkish Cypriot community laws and customs are dictated by the rules of the Sunni branch of Islam. The spiritual leader of the Turkish Cypriot community is the *mufti* of Cyprus who acts more as a judge rather than an administrator.

Ethnic Composition: Greeks and Turks are the two major ethnic groups.

Language: Greek, Turkish, and English are the major languages spoken. Both Greek and Turkish are the official languages in the Republic of Cyprus. English is widely used as a second language by most Cypriots. There are three different forms of Greek practiced in Cyprus; the most important form is *demotiki*, the standard form spoken throughout the Greek community in Cyprus and taught in schools. Since 1979 the Latin alphabet has been used instead of Arabic for the Turkish language.

National Emblem: The Cypriot emblem consists of a gold shield displaying a white dove holding an olive branch in its bill. A decorative garland made of large olive branches surrounds the emblem.

National Anthem: *"Imnos pros tin Eleftherian"* ("The Hymn to Liberty")

Money: The Cyprus pound is a paper currency of 100 cents. The Turkish lira of 100 kurus is the legal currency in the TRNC zone. In February 1993, 1 pound was equal to $2.25 in U.S. currency.

Weights and Measures: Although both imperial and metric systems are understood, Cyprus has its own special internal system, for example, 400 *drams* equal 2.8 pounds or 1.27 kilograms; 1 *pic* equals 2 feet or 61 centimeters; and 1 *donum* equals 14,400 square feet or 1,338 square miles.

Population: The 1992 estimate was 714,000. The population density is about 200 persons per sq. mi. (77 persons per sq km); 64 percent urban; 36 percent rural.

Cities:
```
Nicosia . . . . . . . . . . . . . . . . . . . . . . . . . . . . . . . . . . . . . . . . . . . . . . . . . . 171,000
Limassol . . . . . . . . . . . . . . . . . . . . . . . . . . . . . . . . . . . . . . . . . . . . . . . . . 135,400
Larnaca . . . . . . . . . . . . . . . . . . . . . . . . . . . . . . . . . . . . . . . . . . . . . . . . . . . 62,600
Famagusta. . . . . . . . . . . . . . . . . . . . . . . . . . . . . . . . . . . . . . . . . . . . . . . . . . 39,500
```
(Population based on 1990 estimates, except for Famagusta, which is the 1982 estimate.)

GEOGRAPHY

Area: 3,572 sq. mi. (9,251 sq km)

Border: Cyprus is located in the extreme northeastern corner of the Mediterranean Sea, 44 mi. (71 km) south of Turkey, 230 mi. (370 km) north of Egypt, and 65 mi. (105 km) west of Syria. Cyprus is the largest Mediterranean island after Sicily and Sardinia.

Coastline: 334 mi. (538 km)

Land: The narrow limestone Kyrenia Mountains run along the northern coast for about 100 mi. (160 km). Geologically this is an older range. The Troodos Massif (mountains) in the southwest are sparsely inhabited. The Mesaoria, a low plain, lies in between these two mountain ranges from Famagusta Bay on the east to Morphou Bay on the west. Most of the island's cultivable and pastoral area is concentrated in this plain region.

Highest Point: Mount Olympus, 6,403 ft. (1,952 m)

Lowest Point: Sea level

Rivers: There are very few rivers and lakes. The Yialias and the Pedhieos rivers drain eastward across the Mesaoria. Most of the rivers are small channels that swell up during the thaw of spring and early summer.

Forests: The central plain region was once densely forested, but is now almost treeless. Extensive deforestation has created severe problems of soil erosion. Eucalyptus, pine, and acacia are planted in lowland areas to halt soil erosion. As almost 90 percent of the fuel used for cooking and heating in rural areas is wood, there is a severe deforestation problem. Free pasturing of goats in forestlands is restricted.

Aleppo pine, stone pine, cedar, Mediterranean cypress, juniper, Oriental plane, alder, and Olympus dwarf oak are the most common trees. Natural herbs and wildflowers grow in profusion.

Wildlife: Cyprus has a very small number of wild animals. Some endangered animals, like wild sheep, are protected in the Paphos Forest Game Reserve. Bird life includes partridge, quail, snipe, and woodcock. Eagles are common in the mountainous regions.

Climate: The Mediterranean climate is mostly dry, sunny, and healthful. The winters are mild; only the highest peaks of the Troodos Massif are covered with snow. The central plain is hot and dry in summer; temperatures sometimes go over 100° F. (38° C). The mean annual temperature is about 68° F. (20° C). A cool and rainy season lasts from November to March. Rainfall varies greatly in different parts of the island, from below 12 in. (30 cm) in the west-central lowlands to more than 45 in. (114 cm) in the higher parts of the southern mountains. The central plain receives 12 to 16 in. (30 to 40 cm) of annual rainfall.

Greatest Distance: East to West: 128 mi. (206 km)
North to South: 75 mi. (121 km)

ECONOMY AND INDUSTRY

Agriculture: Cyprus is predominantly an agricultural country. Most of the family farms are small and sometimes scattered within different villages. The chief agricultural products are citrus fruits (grapefruit, tangerines, oranges, and lemons), potatoes, olives, grapes, chick peas, tomatoes, artichokes, watermelons, wheat, and barley. Most of the citrus fruits are grown with irrigation and are exported. Olive oil is a major export. Grapes are processed in the local wineries. Livestock includes goats, poultry, cattle, sheep, and hogs. Fishing is of minor importance to the economy.

Mining: Historically Cyprus produced much copper, but now the mines are almost exhausted. The chief minerals are asbestos, gypsum, iron pyrites, bentonite, umber, and chromite.

Manufacturing: Import duties on raw minerals have been removed to boost manufacturing in Cyprus. Taxes have been almost eliminated to attract foreign investments. Wine, cement, bricks, mosaic tiles, beer, cigarettes, biscuits, margarine, canned fruit and meat, olive oil, textiles, hosiery, pharmaceuticals, and footwear are the chief manufactured products. Energy is derived primarily from imported petroleum. Larnaca has a petroleum refinery.

The redistribution of population in Turkish and Greek sectors has given a boost to construction activity. New hotels are being built to attract tourists.

Transportation: Cyprus has a well-developed road system. There are about 6,090 mi. (9,800 km) of roads, linking all towns and most of the villages. The Greek zone in the south and the Turkish zone in the north have no linking service roads. A private narrow-gauge railway line carries ores from inland mines to loading facilities on the coast. Cyprus Airways is the national carrier; the international airports are at Larnaca and Paphos. Turkish Cypriot Airlines operates in the TRNC and uses Ercan and Gecitkale as international airports. Shipping is an important part of the economy. Cyprus has the world's seventh-largest maritime fleet with two thousand ships sailing under its flag of convenience. Limassol, Paphos, and Larnaca are the chief ports. Good international transportation linkages are essential to the increasingly significant tourist sector of the economy.

Communication: Cyprus Broadcasting Corporation broadcasts mainly in Greek, but also in Turkish, English, and Armenian. Cyprus automatic telecommunications service is ranked among the best in the world. The island has direct dial service to more than 120 nations. In 1990 there were 10 Greek, 8 Turkish, and 1 English daily newspapers, and 3 Greek, 3 Turkish, and 1 English weeklies.

Trade: The chief imports are consumer goods, machinery and transport equipment, aircraft and aircraft parts, plastics and plastic products, paper, metals, chemicals, foodstuffs, and petroleum. The major import sources are the United Kingdom and other European Economic Community (EEC) countries, the United States, and Turkey. The chief exports are clothing, pharmaceutical products, footwear, potatoes, olive oil, and citrus fruits. Major export destinations are Arab countries, the United Kingdom and other EEC countries, and Turkey.

EVERYDAY LIFE

Health: With help from the International Health Division of the Rockefeller Foundation, swamps were drained and malaria has been controlled in most of the rural areas. In the Turkish sector hospitals and clinics are understaffed and sanitation systems are inadequate. In the Greek zone health budgets are substantial.

Education: Cyprus has a well-developed system of primary and secondary education. Elementary education is compulsory and free in both Greek-Cypriot and Turkish-Cypriot regions. Children from 6 to 12 years of age must attend school. Secondary education is voluntary and lasts six years. English and French are compulsory subjects in secondary schools. Technical schools offer options of specialization in classical studies, science, economics, commercial/secretarial, and foreign languages. Technical and vocational colleges provide higher education and training for teachers, technicians, engineers, nurses, and health inspectors. The literacy rate is almost 95 percent. Adult education in Greek rural areas is conducted through youth centers and by Muslim leaders in the Turkish zone.

Holidays:

Holidays observed by the Greek-Cypriot community are:

New Year's Day, January 1
Epiphany, January 6
Green Monday, March 9
Greek Independence Day, March 25
Easter Holiday, movable
Cyprus National Day, April 1
Makarios Memorial Day, August 3
Labor Day, May 1
Cyprus Independence Day (a working holiday), October 1
Greek National Day or "Ohi" Day, October 28
Christmas, December 25

Holidays observed by the Turkish-Cypriot community in TRNC are:

Founding of the Turkish Federated State of Cyprus, February 13
Birthday of the Prophet Muhammad, movable
End of Ramadan, movable
Turkish National Sovereignty and Children's Day, April 23
Turkish Youth and Sports Day, May 19
Peace and Freedom Day, July 20
Communal Resistance Day, August 1
Turkish Victory Day, August 30
Turkish Independence Day, October 1
Turkish Republic Day, October 29
TRNC Day, November 15

Movable Christian and Muslim holidays are observed in the Greek and Turkish zones respectively.

Society: The family unit is very strong throughout Cyprus. Large families are still the custom. Little coffee shops, *kaphenia*, are very popular among Greek men. Women usually visit each other at home. Rural people sometimes wear richly decorated colorful vests and baggy black trousers called *vrakas*. Women generally wear long skirts. Institutional Islam is the foundation of the Turkish Cypriot home life. The Turkish sector's fine crafts are similar to the brass and leather work found in mainland Turkey.

Housing: Cities have large Western-style apartment buildings. Rural people live in simple brick or stone houses; most of the rural architectural style has stayed unchanged since early times. In the lowland areas houses are usually built of sun-dried mud bricks covered with a thin coating of plaster. The roof is flat for drying agricultural products and sleeping in the summer months. The floors are of packed dirt, bricks, mosaics of pebbles, or marble. Rural houses generally consist of three rooms and are built around a courtyard. Simple village buildings are slowly being replaced by suburban-style, two-story, single-family buildings. Within the cities, high-rise buildings are becoming increasingly common. Most of the churches and mosques are more than a hundred years old.

Food: *Klephtiko* is an elaborate feast; mutton or goat meat is slowly cooked in clay ovens. The meat is eaten with bread and vegetable salad. Beer, brandy, and wine are common drinks.

Sports and Recreation: The most popular sport is soccer. Sailing, scuba diving, water skiing, tennis, game shooting, and horseback riding also are popular among tourists and urban dwellers. Mt. Olympus has snow ski facilities. Physical education is part of the school curriculum.

Cards and backgammon are common pastimes for men. Countryside family picnics are enjoyed by the city people. Greek wedding ceremonies are celebrated for two to three days with festivities; everyone in the town is invited.

Aulos, a shepherd's flute, has been in use for music for centuries. Other common musical instruments are violin and *bouzouki*. Dances are performed by pairs of men and pairs of women. Poetry competitions, *chatismata*, are popular at annual fairs.

Social Welfare: A comprehensive social insurance plan covers every working male, female, and their dependents. The program covers unemployment, maternity, sickness, old age, and death.

IMPORTANT DATES

2500 B.C.—Copper mines of Tamaddus are discovered

1200-1050 B.C.—Greek traders establish a Hellenic culture on Cyprus

850 B.C.—Phoenicians settle on Cyprus

498 B.C.—An unsuccessful revolt is staged against the Persians (the culture that occupied the territory of present-day Iran)

333 B.C.—Persian army is defeated by Alexander the Great at the Battle of Issus

294 B.C.—Cyprus is taken by Ptolemy, one of Alexander's generals

c. 15 B.C.—The city of Salamis is destroyed by an earthquake

58 B.C.—Rome annexes Cyprus

A.D. 45 — Apostle Paul and Saint Barnabas bring Christianity to Cyprus

115 — Jewish revolt spreads to Egypt and Cyprus

313 — Edict of Milan proclaims equal rights for all religions

330 — With division of the Roman Empire, Cyprus is incorporated into the Byzantine Empire

333 — Emperor Constantine declares Christianity as the official religion of the Roman Empire

395 — Separation of the administration of Eastern and Western churches is made official

647 or 648 — Syria launches a major naval attack on Cyprus

1191 — Richard the Lionhearted of England captures Cyprus

1192 — Guy de Lusignan establishes an independent dynasty in Cyprus

1489 — Cyprus is ceded to the Venetian Republic

1572 — Cyprus is conquered by the Ottoman Turks; 20,000 Nicosians are killed

1821 — Archbishop Kyprianos and hundreds of priests, accused of plotting a rebellion, are murdered; Greek nationalists revolt in the mainland against the Ottoman Empire

1835 — Nicosia suffers a serious epidemic of cholera

1853 — Crimean War begins (ends 1856)

1857 — Nicosia suffers a severe fire

1878 — Great Britain assumes administration of Cyprus, which remains formally part of the Ottoman Empire

1907 — Asbestos is mined for the first time at Pano Amiandos

1909 — Agricultural cooperative movement begins in Cyprus

1914 — Cyprus is annexed by Britain in consequence of outbreak of war with Turkey

1920-22 — Greco-Turkish War

1924 — Treaty of Lausanne; Turkey renounces claim to Cyprus in favor of Britain

1925 — Great Britain declares Cyprus a crown colony of the British Empire

1931 — Mob violence grips Cyprus; the constitution is suspended

1940 — Axis powers invade Greece

1943 — The first municipal elections since 1931 are held

1947 — British government announces plans to liberalize colonial rule in Cyprus. The land code that existed from the time of the Ottomans is changed by the British; private ownership of land is recognized. The bishop of Kyrenia is elected as head of the Cypriot church

1950 — A plebiscite about union with Greece is held; Makarios II dies and is succeeded by the bishop of Kition as Makarios III

1952 — Makarios III makes his first appearance before the United Nations to present the results of the January enosis plebiscite. Makarios III meets Colonel George Grivas

1954 — United Nations (UN) Security Council turns down Makarios' proposal to discuss the Cyprus problem; widespread rioting begins in Cyprus

1955 — A guerrilla war against Britain begins. Britain declares a state of emergency on the island. A shipful of dynamite is seized by a British destroyer. The Tripartite Conference is held in London

1956 — Official talks are held between Makarios III and the British Governor John Harding; Archbishop Makarios III is exiled to the Seychelles islands by the British

1959 — Greece and Turkey meet in Zurich, Switzerland, and London; Archbishop Makarios III is elected the country's first president

1960 — Cyprus gains independence as a republic; the constitution written by Britain, Greece, and Turkey takes effect; the first elections to the House of Representatives are held

1963 — Makarios is elected president. Thirteen proposals to amend the constitution are put forward by Archbishop Makarios; Turks withdraw from the central government in dispute over constitutional amendments; violence erupts in Nicosia

1964 — Cyprus assumes command of the Cypriot National Guard; the United Nations peacekeeping force reaches Cyprus; some 20,000 to 25,000 Turkish Cypriots are moved to Turkish dominated areas in the north

1967 — Fazil Kucuk declares the "Provisional Cyprus-Turkish Administration"; three Greek generals stage a coup in Greece and establish a military dictatorship

1968 — Makarios is reelected president by an overwhelming majority

1973 — Makarios is reelected president

1974 — Death of Grivas; Makarios is overthrown by National Guard troops led by conspirators from the mainland; he escapes to London. Nicos Sampson is named head of state. Turkish army invades Cyprus and occupies the northern third of the country including part of Nicosia. Makarios returns to Cyprus in December and is reinstated as president. Nicosia airport and Famagusta port are closed for international traffic.

1975 — The northern sector proclaims itself the Turkish Federated State of Cyprus. Turkish lira is adopted as legal currency in Turkish Federated State of Cyprus

1977 — Makarios dies and is succeeded by Spyros Kyprianou as president

1981 — General elections are held under new electoral system

1983 — The northern sector declares independence as the Turkish Republic of Northern Cyprus; Turkish lira replaces Cyprus pound in the northern section; it is recognized only by Turkey. Kyprianou is reelected president in the southern sector

1984 — Diplomatic links are established between Turkey and TRNC. A constitution is drawn for the TRNC by a constituent assembly

1985 — Kyprianou and Denktash hold a meeting but no agreement is reached. The House of Representatives is dissolved and general elections are held in Greek-Cypriot zone. TRNC approves the new constitution by a referendum

1988 — Georghios Vassiliou is elected president

1990 — The government of Cyprus applies for the membership in the European Community; the Turkish Republic of Northern Cyprus opposes the entry. Passport formalities with Turkey are abolished in the TRNC

1992 — The United Nations Security Council adopts a resolution concerning the framework for an agreement on Cyprus

IMPORTANT PEOPLE

Alexander III, called the Great (356-323 B.C.), king of Macedonia; conquered the Persian Empire

Anthemius, Archbishop of Cyprus who gained special privileges for the Church of Cyprus from Emperor Zenon

Barnabas (1st century A.D.), a convert to Christianity and an apostle; accompanied Apostle Paul on his first missionary journey

Mustafa Cagatay, a Turkish-Cypriot leader

Archbishop Chrysostomos, head of the Church of Cyprus after Makarios III

Marcus Tullius Cicero (106-43 B.C.), Roman orator, statesman, philosopher, and leader

Glafkos Clerides, president of the Cypriot House of Representatives; became president after Nikos Sampson

Isaac Comnenos, a Byzantine governor who declared himself King of Cyprus; reigned from 1184 to 1191; defeated by Richard the Lionhearted

Constantine I, called the Great (?280-337), Roman emperor from 306 to 337

King Darius, called the Great (550-486 B.C.), Achaemenid king of Persia (now Iran)

Rauf Denktash (1924-   ), leader of the Turkish Cypriot community; elected vice-president of Cyprus in 1973; became president of the Turkish Federated State of Cyprus in 1975, and of the Turkish Republic of Northern Cyprus in 1983

Dr. Dervis Eroglu, president of the TRNC in 1984

Hugh Foot, British governor of Cyprus

Polykarpos Georkajis (-1971), Greek Cypriot minister of the interior in Cyprus

George Grivas (1898-1974), Greek-Cypriot general who led guerrilla war against British

Emperor Hadrian (A.D. 76-138), Roman emperor from 117 to 138

Field Marshal John Harding, British governor of Cyprus in the 1950s

Georghios Iakovou, Greek-Cypriot leader

Pope Innocent III (1160?-1216), Roman pope from 1198 to 1216; ordered submission from the Cyprus bishops

Colonel Ioannides, Greek leader of 1973 military coup

Constantinos Karamanlis (1907-   ), leader of the democratic government in Greece; prime minister of Greece from 1955 to 1963 and 1974 to 1980 and president of Greece from 1980 to 1985

Nejat Konuk, prime minister of the TFSC from 1976 to 1978

Dr. Fazil Kucuk, the first Turkish vice-president of the Republic of Cyprus

Spyros Kyprianou (1932-   ), head of the Democratic party; president of the House of Representatives from 1976 to 1978; elected as president in 1978 and 1983

Makarios II (-1950), bishop of Kyrenia, elected as the head of the Cypriot church

Makarios III (1913-77), born as Michael Christodoulos Mouskos; ordained a priest in 1946; archbishop; a leader in the struggle for independence; elected the first president of Cyprus in 1959; reelected in 1968 and 1973

Constantine Mitsotakis, conservative Greek prime minister

Mu'awiya (c.602-680), prince of Syria in the 630s; launched a massive naval attack on Cyprus

Muhammad (570-632), prophet and founder of Islam

George Papadopoulos, Greek general who made himself prime minister of Greece by force

Saint Paul (-d. between 62 and 68), a Christian apostle

Ptolemy (?364-283? B.C.), one of Alexander's generals

Richard the Lionhearted (1157-99), king of England from 1189 to 1199; a Crusader

Nicos Sampson, a newspaper publisher, became president for a week

Georghios Vassiliou, a Greek-Cypriot economist and leader; became president in 1988

Zeno of Kition (335?-263? B.C.), philosopher and founder of Stoicism from the pre-Christian world

INDEX

Page numbers that appear in boldface type indicate illustrations

About the Author

Mary Virginia Fox was graduated from Northwestern University in Evanston, Illinois, and now lives near Madison, Wisconsin, across the lake from the state capitol and the University of Wisconsin. She is the author of more than two dozen books for young adults and has had a number of articles published in adult publications.

Mrs. Fox and her husband have lived overseas for several months at a time and enjoy traveling. She considers herself a professional writer and an amateur artist. She has also written *Bahrain, Tunisia, New Zealand,* and *Iran* in the Enchantment of the World series.